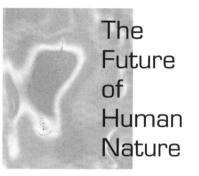

The
Future
of
Human
Nature

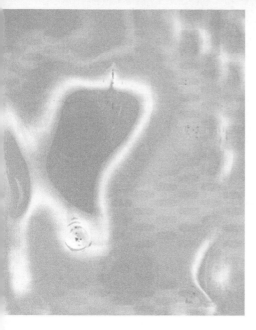

The
Future
of
Human
Nature

JÜRGEN HABERMAS

polity

Chapter 1 was first published as "Begründete Enthaltsamkeit. Gibt es postmetaphysische Antworten auf die Frage nach dem 'richtigen Leben'?" in *Die Zukunft der menschlichen Natur. Auf dem Weg zu einer liberalen Eugenik?*, © Suhrkamp Verlag, Frankfurt am Main 2001. Chapter 2 was first published as "Auf dem Weg zu einer liberalen Eugenik? Der Streit um das ethische Selbstverständnis der Gattung" in *Die Zukunft der menschlichen Natur. Auf dem Weg zu einer liberalen Eugenik?*, © Suhrkamp Verlag, Frankfurt am Main 2001. Chapter 3 was first published as "Glauben und Wissen" in *Friedenspreis des Deutschen Buchhandels 2001*, © Suhrkamp Verlag, Frankfurt am Main 2001.

First published in 2003 by Polity Press in association with Blackwell Publishing Ltd

Editorial office:
Polity Press
65 Bridge Street
Cambridge CB2 1UR, UK

Marketing and production:
Blackwell Publishing Ltd
108 Cowley Road
Oxford OX4 1JF, UK

Distributed in the USA by
Blackwell Publishing Inc.
350 Main Street
Malden, MA 02148, USA

ISBN 0-7456-2986-5
ISBN 0-7456-2987-3 (pb) only available in the UK

A catalogue record for this book is available from the British Library and has been applied for from the Library of Congress.

Typeset in 11 on 13 pt Berling
by SNP Best-set Typesetter Ltd., Hong Kong
Printed and bound in Great Britain by
TJ International, Padstow, Cornwall

For further information on Polity, visit our website: www.polity.co.uk

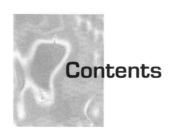

Contents

Publisher's Note

Chapter 1 was translated by William Rehg. The foreword and the postscript to chapter 2 were translated by Max Pensky. The main body of chapters 2 and 3 was translated by Hella Beister and Max Pensky. For the German origins of these chapters, please see details on the copyright page.

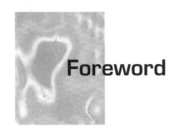

Foreword

On the occasion of receiving the Dr Margrit Egnér Prize for the year 2000, I delivered a lecture on September 9 of that year at the University of Zurich that served as the basis for the first of the texts reproduced here. I proceed on the basis of a distinction between a Kantian theory of justice and a Kierkegaardian ethics of subjectivity, and defend the restraint that postmetaphysical thinking exercises regarding binding positions on substantive questions of the good or the un-misspent life. This is the contrasting background for an opposing question that arises in light of the debates touched off by genetic technology: Can philosophy tolerate this same restraint in questions of a species ethics as well?

The main text, an expanded version of the Christian Wolf Lecture given at Marburg University on June 28, 2001, is an entrance into this debate that does not relinquish the premises of postmetaphysical thinking. So far, this debate over genetic research and technology has circled around the question of the moral status of prepersonal human life without results. I therefore adopt the perspective of a future present, from which we might someday perhaps look back on currently controversial practices as the first steps toward a liberal eugenics regulated by supply and demand. Embryonic research and preimplantation genetic diagnosis excite strong emotions above all because they exemplify a danger that is bound to the metaphor of "human breeding." Not without reason, we worry over the possible emergence of a thick intergenerational web of actions for which no one can be called to account, because it one-sidedly cuts vertically through the contemporary network of interactions. Therapeutic goals, by contrast, on which all genetic technological procedures ought to be based, draw narrow boundaries for each and every intervention. From the therapeutic perspective, one must assume an attitude toward a second person whose consent has to be taken into account.

The postscript to the main text, written at year's end, responds to objections less as a revision than as a clarification of my original intentions.

The third text is based on a speech I delivered on October 14, 2001, on the occasion of my reception of the Peace Prize of the German Book Trade. It takes up a question that has gained new relevance in the wake of September 11: What does an ongoing "secularization" within already secularized societies demand of the citizens of a democratic constitutional state, that is, from the faithful and the unfaithful alike?

Starnberg, December 31, 2001

Are There Postmetaphysical Answers to the Question: What is the "Good Life"?

In the novel *Stiller* Max Frisch has Stiller, the public prosecutor, ask: "What does a human being do with the time he has to live? I was hardly fully aware of the question; it was simply an irritation." Frisch poses the question in the indicative mood. In their self-concern, reflective readers give the question an ethical turn: "What should I do with the time I have to live?" For long enough philosophers believed that they could give suitable advice in reply. But today, in our postmetaphysical age, philosophy no longer pretends to have answers to questions regarding the personal, or even the collective, conduct of life. Theodor Adorno's *Minima Moralia* begins with a melancholy refrain of Nietzsche's "joyful science" – by admitting this inability: "The melancholy science from which I make this offering to my friend relates to a region that from time immemorial was regarded as the true field of philosophy . . . : the teaching of the good life."[1] But ethics has now regressed, as Adorno believed, and become the "melancholy science," because it allows, at best, only scattered, aphoristic "reflections from damaged life."

As long as philosophers still had faith that they were able

1

to assure themselves about their ability to discuss the whole of nature and history, they had authority over the supposedly established frameworks into which the human life of individuals and communities had to fit. The order of the cosmos and human nature, the stages of secular and sacred history provided normatively laden facts that, so it seemed, could also disclose the right way to live. Here "right" had the exemplary sense of an imitation-worthy model for living, both for the life of the individual and for the political community. Just as the great religions present their founders' way of life as the path to salvation, so also metaphysics offered its models of life – for the select few, of course, who did not follow the crowd. The doctrines of the good life and of a just society – ethics and politics – made up a harmonious whole. But with the acceleration of social change, the lifespans of these models of the good life have become increasingly shorter – whether they were aimed at the Greek polis, the estates of the medieval *societas civilis*, the well-rounded individual of the urban Renaissance or, as with Hegel, at the system of family, civil society, and constitutional monarchy.

Rawls's political liberalism marks the endpoint of this development, precisely as a response to the pluralism of worldviews and to the spreading individualization of lifestyles. Surveying the rubble of philosophical attempts to designate *particular* ways of life as exemplary or universally obligatory, Rawls draws the proper conclusion: that the "just society" ought to leave it to individuals to choose how it is that they want to "spend the time they have for living." It guarantees to each an equal freedom to develop an ethical self-understanding, so as to realize a personal conception of the "good life" according to one's own abilities and choices.

It is certainly true that individual life-projects do not emerge independently of intersubjectively shared life contexts. However, in complex societies one culture can assert itself against other cultures only by convincing its succeeding generations – who can also say no – of the advan-

2

tages of its world-disclosive semantic and action-orienting power. "Nature reserves" for cultures are neither possible nor desirable. In a constitutional democracy the majority may also not prescribe for minorities aspects of its own cultural form of life (beyond the common political culture of the country) by claiming for its culture an authoritative guiding function (as "*Leitkultur*").

As the foregoing remarks indicate, practical philosophy by no means renounces all of its normative concerns. At the same time, it does restrict itself, by and large, to questions of justice. In particular, its aim is to clarify the moral point of view from which we judge norms and actions whenever we must determine what lies in the equal interest of everyone and what is equally good for all. At first glance, moral theory and ethics appear to be oriented to the same question: What ought I, or what ought we, to do? But the "ought" has a different sense once we are no longer asking about rights and duties that everyone ascribes to one another from an inclusive we-perspective, but instead are concerned with our own life from the first-person perspective and ask what is best "for me" or "for us" in the long run and all things considered. Such ethical questions regarding our own weal and woe arise in the context of a *particular* life history or a *unique* form of life. They are wedded to questions of identity: how we should understand ourselves, who we are and want to be. Obviously there is no answer to such questions that would be independent of the given context and thus would bind all persons in the same way.

Consequently, theories of justice and morality take their own separate path today, at least a path different from that of "ethics," if we understand this in the classical sense of a doctrine of the right way to live. The moral point of view obliges us to abstract from those exemplary pictures of a successful or undamaged life that have been handed on in the grand narratives of metaphysics and religion. Our existential self-understanding can still continue to draw its nourishment from the substance of these traditions just as

3

it always did, but philosophy no longer has the right to intervene in this struggle of gods and demons. Precisely with regard to the questions that have the greatest relevance for us, philosophy retires to a metalevel and investigates only the formal properties of processes of self-understanding, without taking a position on the contents themselves. That may be unsatisfying, but who can object to such a well-justified reluctance?

To be sure, moral theory pays a high price for its division of labor with an ethics that specializes in the forms of existential self-understanding: it thereby dissolves the context that first linked moral judgments with the motivation toward right action. Moral insights effectively bind the will only when they are embedded in an ethical self-understanding that joins the concern about one's own well-being with the interest in justice. Deontological theories after Kant may be very good at explaining how to ground and apply moral norms; but they still are unable to answer the question of why we should be moral *at all*. Political theories are likewise unable to answer the question of why the citizens of a democratic polity, when they disagree about the principles of their living together, should orient themselves toward the common good – and not rather satisfy themselves with a strategically negotiated modus vivendi. Theories of justice that have been uncoupled from ethics can only *hope* that processes of socialization and political forms of life meet them halfway.[2]

Even more disquieting is a further question: Why should philosophical ethics give way to psychotherapies that have few qualms about taking on the classical task of providing an orientation for living by eliminating psychic disturbances? The philosophical core of psychoanalysis clearly emerges when, for example, Alexander Mitscherlich understands psychological illness as the impairment of a specifically human mode of existence. Such illness signifies a self-inflicted loss of freedom, because the patient is simply compensating for an unconscious suffering with

4

his symptoms – a suffering he escapes by self-deception. The goal of therapy is a self-knowledge that "is often nothing more than the transformation of illness into suffering, albeit a suffering that raises *Homo sapiens* to a higher level because it does not negate his freedom."[3]

Such a concept of psychological "illness" stems from an analogy with somatic illness. But how far does this analogy go, given that the area of psychology largely lacks observable and clearly ascertainable parameters for health? Evidently a normative understanding of an "undisturbed self-existence" must fill in for the missing somatic indicators. This is especially clear in those cases where the pressure of suffering that drives the patient to the analyst is itself repressed, so that the disturbance inconspicuously fits into a normal life. Why should philosophy shrink back from matters that psychoanalysis, for example, believes it can deal with? This issue concerns the clarification of our intuitive understanding of the clinical aspects of an unsuccessful or not-unsuccessful life. Moreover, the text quoted above from Mitscherlich betrays his debt to the existential philosophy of authors like Kierkegaard and his successors. This is no accident.

Kierkegaard was the first philosopher who answered the basic ethical question regarding the success or failure of one's own life with a postmetaphysical concept of "being-able-to-be-oneself." Kierkegaard's philosophical descendants – Heidegger, Jaspers, and Sartre – found such a radical Protestant's obsession with a merciful God a bit much. In his engagement with Hegel's speculative thought, Kierkegaard answered the question of the right way to live with an answer that was indeed *postmetaphysical*, while at the same time *theological*. But the existentialist philosophers who were committed to a methodological atheism recognized Kierkegaard as the

thinker who revived the ethical question in the most inno-
vative manner and provided an answer that was not only
substantive but also sufficiently formal – sufficiently
formal, that is, in view of a legitimate pluralism of worldviews that prohibits any form of paternalism in the area
of genuinely ethical advice. The Kierkegaard of *Either/Or*,
with his concept of the "ethical stage" of existence, offered
the natural point of conncction.

In contrast to the romantic picture of an egocentrically
playful form of life that is lazily carried along by the
present moment and dominated by reflected pleasure,
Kierkegaard opposes the ethically resolute conduct of life.
The latter demands that I *gather* myself and detach myself
from the dependencies of an overwhelming environment,
jolting myself to the awareness of my individuality and
freedom. Once I am emancipated from a self-induced
objectification, I also gain distance from myself as an individual. I pull myself out from the anonymous, scattered
life that is breathlessly disintegrating into fragments and
give my life continuity and transparency. In the social
dimension, such a person can assume responsibility for his
or her own actions and can enter into binding commit-
ments with others. In the temporal dimension, concern for
oneself makes one conscious of the historicity of an existence that is realized in the simultaneously interpenetrat-
ing horizons of future and past.

Kierkegaard tacitly assumes that as a self-consciously
existing individual, one continuously gives an account of
one's life in light of the Sermon on the Mount. He does
not waste many words on the moral standards themselves,
which found secular expression in Kant's egalitarian
universalism. Rather, all his attention is on the structure
of the ability to be oneself, that is, on the form of an ethical
self-reflection and self-choice that is determined by the
infinite interest in the success of one's own life-project.
With a view toward future possibilities of action, the individual self-critically appropriates the past of her factually
given, concretely re-presented life history. Only then does

she make herself into a person who speaks for herself, an irreplaceable individual.

Such an individual regrets the reproachable aspects of his past life and resolves to continue only in those ways of acting in which he can recognize himself without shame. In this way, he articulates the self-understanding of the person he would like others to know and acknowledge. Through a morally scrupulous evaluation and critically probing appropriation of his factually given life history, he constitutes himself as the person he both is and would like to be:

> Everything that is posited in his freedom belongs to him essentially, however accidental it may seem to be. . . . this distinction is not a product of his arbitrariness so that he might seem to have absolute power to make himself into what it pleased him to be . . . To be sure, the ethical individual dares to employ the expression that he is his own editor, but he is also fully aware that he is responsible, responsible for himself personally . . . responsible to the order of things in which he lives, responsible to God.[4]

Kierkegaard is convinced that the ethical form of existence produced by one's own efforts can be stabilized only in the relation of the believer to God. As long as we ground morality as the standard for self-scrutiny in human knowledge (as in the Socratic or Kantian approaches), the motivation for converting moral judgments into practice is lacking. Kierkegaard objects not so much to the cognitive meaning of morality as to its intellectualistic misunderstanding. If morality could move the will of the knowing subject *solely* through good reasons, then we could not explain that desolate condition against which Kierkegaard as critic of the contemporary age directed his barbs again and again – the condition of an enlightened and morally self-righteous, but deeply corrupt Christian society: "It is tragic-comic to see that all this knowledge and understanding exercises no power at all over men's lives."[5]

7

The cynical acceptance of an unjust world, the normality of repression for so many people, is evidence not of a deficit in *knowledge* but of a corruption of the *will*. The human beings who could know better do not *want* to understand. For this reason, Kierkegaard does not speak of guilt, but of sin. However, as soon as we interpret guilt as sin, we know that we have need of forgiveness and that we must set our hope on an absolute power that can intervene retroactively in the course of history and can *restore* the wounded order as well as the integrity of the victims. The promise of salvation forms the motivating connection between an unconditionally demanding morality and care for oneself. A postconventional morality of conscience can become the seed around which a conscious life conduct thus can crystallize only if it is embedded in a religious self-understanding. Kierkegaard develops the problem of motivation over and against Socrates and Kant in order to go beyond both of them and arrive at Christ.

To be sure, Climacus – Kierkegaard's pseudonymous author of *Philosophical Fragments* – is not at all sure that the Christian message of redemption, which he considers hypothetically as a "project" for thought, is "more true" than the immanent thinking that moves within the postmetaphysical boundaries of neutrality towards worldviews.[6] Thus, Kierkegaard presents Anticlimacus as one who does not try to compel his secular counterpart with argument but aims rather to induce him with the help of a psychological phenomenology "to go beyond Socrates."

Drawing on symptomatic forms of life, Kierkegaard describes the visible forms of a healing "sickness unto death" – the patterns of a despair that is initially repressed, then creeps into awareness, and finally forces conversion on an ego-centered consciousness. These forms of despair are so many manifestations of the lack of a fundamental relationship that alone could make an authentic being-oneself possible. Kierkegaard depicts the unsettling condition of a person who is indeed aware of her destiny, that she must be a self, but thereupon flees into the alternatives: "in despair not to will to be oneself. Or even lower: in despair not to will to be a self. Or lowest of all: in despair to will to be someone else."[7] The one who finally realizes that the despair has its source not in circumstances but in one's own flight responses will make the defiant, but equally unsuccessful attempt "to will to be oneself." The hopeless failure of this last act of will – the stubborn wanting to be oneself entirely on the basis of one's own resources – pushes finite spirit to transcend itself and recognize its dependence on an Other as the ground of its own freedom.

This conversion marks the turning point in the movement of overcoming the secularized self-understanding of modern reason. For Kierkegaard describes this rebirth with a formulation that recalls the opening paragraphs of Fichte's *Wissenschaftslehren,* yet at the same time inverts the autonomous sense of the deed [*Tathandlung*] into its opposite: "In relating itself to itself and in willing to be itself, the self rests transparently in the power that established it."[8] The fundamental relation that makes being-oneself possible as the form of right living thereby becomes visible. Although the literal reference to a "power" as the ground of being-able-to-be-oneself need not be understood in a religious sense, Kierkegaard insists that the human spirit can arrive at a right understanding of its finite existence only through the awareness of sin: the self exists authentically [*wahrhaftig*] only in the presence of God. The self survives the stages of hopeless despair only in the form of a believer, who by relating herself to herself relates to an absolutely Other to whom she owes everything.[9]

Kierkegaard emphasizes that we cannot form any consistent concept of God – neither *via eminentiae* nor *via negationis.* Each idealization remains captive to the basic predicates from which the operation of intensification takes its point of departure. And the attempt of the understanding to characterize the absolutely Other by negating all finite determinations fails for the same reason: "The

9

understanding cannot even think the absolutely different; it cannot absolutely negate itself but uses itself for that purpose and consequently thinks the difference in itself."[10] The chasm between knowing and believing cannot be bridged by thought.

Kierkegaard's philosophical followers naturally find this point annoying. To be sure, even Socratic thinkers who cannot invoke revealed truths can follow the suggestive phenomenology of the "sickness unto death" and can agree that finite spirit depends on enabling conditions beyond its control. The ethically conscious conduct of life should not be understood as narrow-minded self-empowerment. They could also agree with Kierkegaard that we should not understand this dependence on a power beyond our control in naturalistic terms, but above all as an interpersonal relation. For the defiance of a rebellious person who finally in despair wills to be herself is directed – as defiance – against a second person. Under the premises of postmetaphysical thinking, however, the power beyond us – on which we subjects capable of speech and action depend in our concern not to fail to lead worthwhile lives – cannot be identified with "God in time."

The linguistic turn permits a deflationary interpretation of the "wholly Other." As historical and social beings we find ourselves always already in a linguistically structured lifeworld. In the forms of communication through which we reach an understanding with one another about something in the world and about ourselves, we encounter a transcending power. Language is not a kind of private property. No one possesses exclusive rights over the common medium of the communicative practices we must intersubjectively share. No single participant can control the structure, or even the course, of processes of reaching understanding and self-understanding. How speakers and hearers make use of their communicative freedom to take yes- or no-positions is not a matter of their subjective discretion. For they are free only in virtue of the binding force of the justifiable claims they raise toward one another. The *logos* of language embodies the power of the intersubjective, which precedes and grounds the subjectivity of speakers.

This weak proceduralist reading of the "Other" preserves the fallibilist as well as the anti-skeptical meaning of the "unconditioned." The *logos* of language escapes our control, and yet we are the ones, the subjects capable of speech and action, who reach an understanding with one another in this medium. It remains "our" language. The unconditionedness of truth and freedom is a necessary presupposition of our practices, but beyond the constituents of "our" form of life they lack any ontological guarantee. Similarly, the "right" ethical self-understanding is neither revealed nor "given" in some other way. It can only be won in a common endeavor. From this perspective, what makes our being-ourselves possible appears more as a transsubjective power than an absolute one.

Even if we adopt this postreligious perspective, Kierkegaard's postmetaphysical ethics permits us to characterize a not-unsuccessful life. His general statements about the modes of being-able-to-be-oneself are formal – that is, they are not *thick* descriptions – but they by no means lack normative content. Because this ethics judges the existential *mode*, but not the specific orientation of, individual life-projects and particular forms of life, it satisfies the conditions of a pluralism of worldviews. This postmetaphysical abstention runs up against its limits in an interesting way as soon as questions of a "species ethics" arise. As soon as the ethical self-understanding of language-using agents is at stake *in its entirety*, philosophy can no longer avoid taking a substantive position.

It is just this situation that we find ourselves in today. The advance of the biological sciences and development of biotechnologies at the threshold of the new century do not just expand familiar possibilities of action, they enable a new type of intervention. What hitherto was "given" as organic nature, and could at most be "bred," now shifts to the realm of artifacts and their production. To the degree that even the human organism is drawn into this sphere of intervention, Helmuth Plessner's phenomenological distinction between "being a body" and "having a body" becomes surprisingly current: the boundary between the nature that we "are" and the organic endowments we "give" to ourselves disappears.[11] As a result, a new kind of self-transformation, one that reaches into the depth of the organic substrate, emerges for the intervening subject. The self-understanding of this subject now determines how one wants to use the opportunities opened up with this new scope for decision – to proceed *autonomously* according to the standards governing the normative deliberations that enter into democratic will formation, or to proceed *arbitrarily* according to subjective preferences whose satisfaction depends on the market. In putting the question this way, I am not taking the attitude of a cultural critic opposed to welcome advances of scientific knowledge. Rather, I am simply asking whether, and if so how, the implementation of these achievements affects our self-understanding as responsible agents.

Do we want to treat the categorically new possibility of intervening in the human genome as an increase in freedom that requires normative *regulation* – or rather as self-empowerment for transformations that depend simply on our preferences and do not require any *self-limitation*? Even if this fundamental question is decided in favor of the first alternative, one can dispute the boundaries of a negative eugenics that would aim at overcoming unmistakable evils. Here I will only point out one aspect of the underlying problem – the challenge posed by the modern understanding of freedom. The decoding of the human genome opens up the prospect of interventions that cast a peculiar light on a condition of our normative self-understanding, a condition that, although natural and thus far unthematized, now turns out nonetheless to be essential.

Up to now, both the secular thought of European modernity and religious belief could proceed on the assumption that the genetic endowment of the newborn infant, and thus the initial organic conditions for its future life history, lay beyond any programming and deliberate manipulation on the part of other persons. To be sure, adults can submit their own life histories to critical evaluation and retrospective revision. Our life histories are made from a material that we can "make our own" and "responsibly take possession of," in Kierkegaard's sense. What is placed at our disposal today is something else: the previous *uncontrollability* of the contingent process of human fertilization that results from what is now an *unforeseeable* combination of two different sets of chromosomes. However, this rather ordinary contingency proves to be – in the very moment we can master it – a necessary presupposition for being-able-to-be-oneself and for the fundamentally egalitarian nature of our interpersonal relationships. For as soon as adults treat the desirable genetic traits of their descendants as a product they can shape according to a design of their own liking, they are exercising a kind of control over their genetically manipulated offspring that intervenes in the somatic bases of another person's spontaneous relation-to-self and ethical freedom. This kind of intervention should only be exercised over things, not persons. For this reason, later generations can demand an account from the programmers of their genome; they can hold these producers responsible for what they, the offspring, consider the unwanted consequences of the organic starting point of their life histories. This new structure of attribution results from obliterating the boundary between persons and things. One can see this, for example, in the case of the parents of a handicapped child who hold their physician responsible for the material consequences of a mistaken prenatal diagnosis and undertake a civil suit for "compensatory damages" – as though the medically unexpected handicap were tantamount to damage to one's property.

A previously unheard-of interpersonal relationship arises when a person makes an irreversible decision about the natural traits of another person. This new type of relationship offends our moral sensibility because it constitutes a foreign body in the legally institutionalized relations of recognition in modern societies. When one person makes an irreversible decision that deeply intervenes in another's organic disposition, the fundamental symmetry of responsibility that exists among free and equal persons is restricted. We have a fundamentally different kind of freedom toward the fate produced through the contingencies of our socialization than we would have toward the prenatal production of our genome. The developing adolescent will one day be able to take responsibility for her own life history; she will be able to take possession of what she is. That is, she can relate to her process of development reflectively, work out a *revisionary* self-understanding, and in a probing manner retrospectively restore the balance to the asymmetrical responsibility that parents have for their children's upbringing. This possibility of a self-critical appropriation of one's own developmental history is not available in regard to genetically manipulated dispositions. Rather, the adult would remain blindly dependent on the nonrevisable decision of another person, without any opportunity to establish the symmetrical responsibility required if one is to enter into a retroactive ethical self-reflection as a process among *peers*. For this poor soul there are only two alternatives, fatalism and resentment.

Would this situation change significantly if we expanded the scenario of the embryo's objectification in favor of the adult's self-objectifying correction of her *own* genome? In this case as in the previous one, the consequences show that the breadth of biotechnological interventions raises moral questions that are not simply difficult in the familiar sense but are of an *altogether different kind*.

The answers touch on the ethical self-understanding of humanity as a whole. The European Union's Charter of Basic Rights that was agreed to in Nice already takes into consideration the circumstance that procreation and birth are losing the element of natural uncontrollability that so far was essential for our normative self-understanding. Article 3, which guarantees the right to bodily and mental integrity, contains "the prohibition against eugenic practices, especially those that have as their goal the selection of persons," as well as "the prohibition against the reproductive cloning of human beings."[12] But have not these traditional European value orientations, however worthy, already become merely out-of-date fashions?

Do we still want to understand ourselves as normative creatures – indeed, what role should morality and law play in the regulation of social interaction that could as well get rearranged in norm-free functionalist terms? Naturalistic alternatives are currently under discussion. These alternatives include not only the reductionistic proposals of natural scientists but also the adolescent speculations about the superior artificial intelligence of future generations of robots.

As a result, the ethics of *successfully being oneself* has become one among several alternatives. Formal arguments no longer suffice to maintain the substance of this self-understanding in the face of competing proposals. Rather, today the original philosophical question concerning the "good life" in all its anthropological generality appears to have taken on new life. The new technologies make a public discourse on the right understanding of cultural forms of life in general an urgent matter. And philosophers no longer have any good reasons for leaving such a dispute to biologists and engineers intoxicated by science fiction.

The Debate on the Ethical Self-Understanding of the Species

> If the prospective parents sue for an extensive degree
> of self-determination, it would be only right and proper
> for the future child to be also guaranteed the opportu-
> nity to lead an autonomous life.
>
> Andreas Kuhlmann, *Politik des Lebens,*
> *Politik des Sterbens*

In 1973, scientists succeeded in separating and redesign-
ing elementary components of a genome. Ever since this
artificial recombination of genes, genetic engineering has
accelerated, especially in the field of reproduction medicine, developments which had set in with the procedures
of prenatal diagnosis and, since 1978, in vitro fertilization.
With the procedure of in vitro fusion of egg cell and
sperm cell, human embryonic stem cells are available
for extrauterine experimentation. "Assisted Reproductive
Technology," it is true, already gave rise to practices intervening in a spectacular way in intergenerational relations,
that is the conventional relationship of social parenthood
and biological descent. I am thinking of surrogate mothers
and anonymous gamete donation, of postmenopausal
pregnancy made possible by egg donation or of the per-
versely delayed use made of frozen egg cells. But it took
the combined efforts of reproduction medicine and

16

genetic engineering to generate the procedures of pre-implantation genetic diagnosis (PGD) and open up the prospect of organ breeding and gene-modifying interventions for therapeutic goals. Today, even the general public confronts questions whose moral weight greatly exceeds the substance of ordinary matters of political dispute. What, then, is at stake?

Preimplantation genetic diagnosis permits genetic screening to be carried out on embryos at the eight-cell stage. This procedure is recommended, in the first place, to parents wanting to rule out the risk of transmitting a hereditary disease. If found to be deficient, the embryo screened in the test-tube will not be implanted in the mother, thus sparing her an abortion at a later stage as a result of prenatal diagnosis. In the same line, *research on totipotent stem cells* is by now understood in terms of proactive medical care. Hypothesizing on future developments, scientific research, pharma business, and industrial location policy will have us believe that they will soon be able to overcome the bottlenecks of organ procurement for transplantation surgery by breeding organ-specific tissue from embryonic stem cells and, in the long run, to cure severe diseases due to monogenetic causes by intervening in, and correcting, the genome itself. In Germany, pressure to reenact the as yet unrepealed law for the protection of embryos is increasing. The German Science Foundation substantiates its claim to privilege freedom of research over the protection of the life of the embryo and "not to explicitly create, but use early stages of human life for research purposes" by invoking the high-ranking goal and "realistic opportunity" of developing new treatments.

However, the authors themselves appear to be doubtful as to the validity of such reasons derived from the "logic of healing." Otherwise, they would not have given up the participant perspective of normative discourse to take refuge in the observer position. As it is, referring to the long-term preservation of artificially fertilized egg cells, licit use of nidation obstacles (intrauterine devices preventing not conception, but nidation) and existing abortion regulations, they go on to say that "the Rubicon, here, was crossed with the introduction of artificial insemination, and it would be hardly realistic to believe that in a context of existing decisions on the embryo's right to live, our society might return to the *status quo ante*." As a sociological prediction, this may well turn out to be true. But as part of a moral reflection on legal policy, reference to the normative force of established facts will only confirm a skeptical public's fear that science, technology, and economics may create, by their systemic dynamics, *faits accomplis* which can outstrip any normative framework. The half-hearted maneuver of the German Science Foundation disavows the appeasement policy of a research field which already largely relies on the capital market for funding. As biotechnological research is by now bound up with investors' interests as well as with the pressure for success felt by national governments, the development of genetic engineering has acquired a dynamic which threatens to steamroll the inherently slow-paced processes of an ethicopolitical opinion and will formation in the public sphere.[1]

Processes of reaching a political self-understanding, being time-consuming by nature, are most at risk from a lack of perspectives. They have to avoid being tied down to the technological and regulatory needs of the moment, and instead must let themselves be guided by a comprehensive perspective on future developments. The following scenario of medium-range development, for instance, might be far from unlikely. As a first step, the population in general as well as the political public sphere and parliament may come to feel that preimplantation genetic diagnosis *as such* may be morally permitted or legally tolerated if limited to a small number of well-defined cases of severe hereditary diseases which *the persons who are potentially affected by them in the future cannot be reasonably expected to cope with*. With the advances of biotechnology, and with gene therapy meeting with success,

18

regulations will later be extended to cover genetic intervention in somatic cells (or even in the germ line)[2] for the purpose of preventing such (and similar) hereditary diseases. This second step which, given the choice made in the first place, is not only non-objectionable but consistent, leads to the necessity of drawing a line between these "negative" eugenics (assumed to be justified) and "positive" eugenics (still considered problematic). But since this line is not sharp – both on conceptual and practical grounds – our intention of making genetic interventions *stop* at the threshold of enhancing human beings confronts us with a paradoxical challenge: in the very dimensions where boundaries are fluid, we are supposed to draw and to enforce particularly clear-cut lines. Even now this argument is used in defense of liberal eugenics, which, while refusing to accept the distinction between therapeutic and enhancing interventions, leaves the choice of the goals of gene-modifying interventions to the individual preferences of market participants.[3]

Such may well have been the scenario which the President of the Federal Republic of Germany, Johannes Rau, had in mind when he spoke out on May 18 to utter a warning: "Once you start to instrumentalize human life, once you start to distinguish between life worth living and life not worth living, you embark on a course where there is no stopping point."[4] The "floodgates argument" sounds less alarmist if one considers the way in which accidental precedents and inconspicuous practices which (like prenatal diagnosis today) have become ingrained through normalization are retrospectively exploited, by those lobbying for genetic engineering and biotechnology, in order to shrug off moral misgivings as "too late." The correct way, methodologically speaking, of using that argument would imply that we are well advised to control any normative judgment of ongoing developments by referring to issues which, due to the potential developments of genetic engineering and biotechnology (and notwithstanding the experts' assurances of their being as yet quite out of reach), we may some day be confronted with.[5] It is not dramatization I seek in invoking this maxim. As long as we consider in time the more dramatic borderlines which the day after tomorrow might be crossed, we can approach today's problems with more composure – and all the more readily admit that one may indeed be hard put to it to substantiate alarmist reactions by compelling moral reasons; such reasons, as I see them, being secular ones which in a society with a pluralistic outlook may reasonably be expected to meet with a rather general acceptance.

Application of preimplantation technology is bound up with the normative question of "whether the fact that one was conditionally created and had one's right to existence and development depend on genetic screening is consistent with the dignity of human life."[6] May we feel free to dispose over human life for the purposes of selection? A similar question is raised by the perspective of "using" embryos with the vague prospect of some day being able to breed (from one's own body cells as well) and to implant transplantable tissues (thus forestalling the problem of having to overcome the immune response against alien cells). To the extent that the creation and destruction of embryos for the purposes of medical research are extended and normalized, the cultural perception of antenatal human life will change, too, blunting our moral sensibility for the limits of cost-benefit analyses in general. Today, we are still sensitive to the obscenity of this reifying practice, and wonder whether we want to live in a society which is ready to swap sensitivity regarding the normative and natural foundations of its existence for the narcissistic indulgence of our own preferences.

In the perspective of the self-instrumentalization and self-optimization to which humanity is about to subject the biological foundations of its existence, both issues, PGD and stem cell research, become part of the same context. This sheds a light on the inconspicuous normative interplay between the *inviolability* of the person, which is imperative on moral grounds and subject to legal guarantees, and the natural mode of the person's physical embodiment, which is something we cannot dispose over.

Even today, preimplantation genetic diagnosis is hard put to it to strictly keep to the line separating the selection of undesirable hereditary factors from the optimization of desirable ones. If there is more than one potentially "spare multicellular organism" to be chosen among, the decision implied is no longer a binary one of yes or no. The conceptual distinction between the prevention of the birth of a severely afflicted child and the optimization of the genetic makeup, that is, a eugenic choice, has become blurred.[7] The practical importance of this will become evident as soon as more far-reaching expectations, namely interventions correcting the human genome, are realized, enabling us to prevent diseases due to monogenetic causes. The conceptual problem of distinguishing between prevention and eugenics will then become a matter of political legislation. If we consider that medical mavericks are already busy working on the reproductive cloning of human organisms, we cannot help but feel that the human species might soon be able to take its biological evolution into its own hands.[8] "Partner in evolution" or even "playing God" are the metaphors for an *auto-transformation of the species* which it seems will soon be within reach.

Of course, this is not the first time that a theory of evolution has sparked proposals and suggestions that intrude into the lifeworld and affect the associative horizon of public discourse. What seems to be returning today, against a background of globalized neoliberalism, is the explosive alliance of Darwinism and free trade ideology, an alliance which flourished at the turn of the twentieth century under the banner of the Pax Britannica. The issue today, of course, is no longer the overgeneralization of biological insights by social Darwinists, but rather the weakening of the "sociomoral restrictions" placed on biotechnological progress for medical as well as economic reasons. This is the front line where the political convictions of Gerhard Schröder and Johannes Rau, the Liberal Party and the "Green Party" are now in conflict.

Nor is there, to be sure, any lack of wild speculation. A handful of freaked-out intellectuals is busy reading the tea leaves of a naturalistic version of posthumanism, only to give, at what they suppose to be a time-wall, one more spin – "hypermodernity" against "hypermorality" – to the all-too-familiar motives of a very German ideology.[9] Fortunately, the elitist dismissals of "the illusion of egalitarianism" and the discourse of justice still lack the power for large-scale infection. Self-styled Nietzscheans, indulging in fantasies of the "battle between large-scale and small-scale man-breeders" as "the fundamental conflict of all future," and encouraging the "main cultural factions" to "exercise the power of selection which they have actually gained," have, so far, succeeded only in staging a media spectacle.[10] As an alternative, I will appeal to the more sober premises of the constitutional state in a pluralistic society,[11] as a way of contributing to some clarification of our confused moral sentiments.[12]

Quite literally, however, this essay is an *attempt*, seeking to attain more transparence for a rather mixed-up set of intuitions. I am personally far from believing that I have succeeded, be it halfway, in this pursuit. But neither do I see any analyses of a more convincing nature.[13] What is so unsettling is the fact that the dividing line between the nature we *are* and the organic equipment we *give* ourselves is being blurred. My perspective in this examination of the current debate over the need to regulate genetic engineering is therefore guided by the question of the meaning, for our own life prospects and for our self-understanding as moral beings, of the proposition that the genetic foundations of our existence should not be disposed over (I). The well-known arguments taken from the abortion debate, I believe, set the wrong course. The right to an unmanipulated genetic heritage is not at all the same issue as the regulation of abortion (II). Gene manipulation is bound up with issues touching upon the identity of the species, while such an anthropological self-understanding provides the context in which our conceptions of law and of morality are embedded (III). My particular concern is with the question of how the biotechnological dedifferentiation of the habitual distinction between the "grown" and the "made", the subjective and the objective, may change our ethical self-understanding as members of the species (IV) and affect the self-understanding of a genetically programmed person (V). We cannot rule it out that knowledge of one's own hereditary features as programmed may prove to restrict the choice of an individual's way of life, and to undermine the essentially symmetrical relations between free and equal human beings (VI). Research involving the destruction of embryos and preimplantation genetic diagnosis will provoke passionate responses because they are perceived to exemplify the very dangers of liberal eugenics we may soon be confronted with (VII).

Moralizing human nature?

Due to the spectacular advances of molecular genetics, more and more of what we are "by nature" is coming within the reach of biotechnological intervention. From the perspective of experimental science, this technological control of human nature is but another manifestation of our tendency to extend continuously the range of what we can control within our natural environment. From a life-world perspective, however, our attitude changes as soon as this extension of our technological control crosses the line between "outer" and "inner" nature. In Germany, legislators have banned not only PGD and research involving the destruction of embryos, but also therapeutic cloning, "surrogate motherhood," and "medically assisted suicide" which have been legalized in other countries. Regarding technological interventions in the germ line and the cloning of human organisms, ostracism is so far still world-wide, and obviously not only because of the risks they involve. In this we may see, with W. van den Daele, an attempt at "moralizing human nature": "That which science made technologically manipulable reacquires, from a normative perspective, its character as something we may not control."[14]

Throughout modern times, new technological developments have created new regulatory needs. To date, however, changes in normative regulations have been produced as adaptations to societal transformations. It has always been social change, resulting from technological innovations in the fields of production and exchange, communication and transport, the military, and medicine, which took the lead. Even the posttraditional conceptions of law and morality have been described by classical social theories as a product of cultural and societal rationalization acting *in the same direction* as the advances of modern science and technology. Institutionalized research was perceived as the driving force behind this progress. From the perspective of the liberal state, the freedom of science and research is entitled to legal guarantees. Any enhancement of the scope and focus of the technological control of nature is bound up with the economic promise of gains in productivity and increasing prosperity, as well as with the political prospect of enlarging the scope for individual choice. And since enlarging the scope of individual choice fosters individual autonomy, science and technology have, to date, formed an evident alliance with the fundamental credo of liberalism, holding that all citizens are entitled to equal opportunities for an autonomous direction of their own lives.

From the sociological perspective, it is unlikely that society's acceptance of this will lessen, as long as the instrumentalization of humanity's inner nature can be medically justified by the prospect of better health and a prolonged lifespan. The wish to be autonomous in the conduct of one's own life is always connected with the collective goals of health and the prolongation of lifespan. The history of medicine, therefore, strongly suggests a skeptical attitude toward any attempt at "moralizing human nature":

> Time and again, from the beginning of vaccination and the first attempts at heart and brain surgery, going on to organ transplantation and the breeding of artificial organs and coming up again, today, with gene therapy, there have been debates over whether or not a limit had been reached, beyond which further extension of the instrumentalization of man cannot be justified even by clinical purposes. None of these debates has stopped technology.[15]

From this sober empirical perspective, legislative interventions restricting the freedom of biological research and banning the advances of genetic engineering seem but a vain attempt to set oneself against the dominant tendency to freedom of modern society.[16] "Moralizing human nature," here, is perceived in terms of a rather dubious sanctification. After science and technology have, at the expense of a desocialization or disenchantment of outer nature, enlarged the scope of our freedom, this irresistible tendency is now to be brought to a standstill, it seems, by erecting artificial barriers in terms of taboos, that is, by a reenchantment of inner nature.

The implicit recommendation in this is obvious: we had better elucidate the archaic remnants of emotions which may linger in our revulsion before the prospect of chimera created by genetic engineering, at bred and cloned human beings, and at embryos being destroyed in the course of experimentation. A quite different scenario, however, emerges if "moralizing human nature" is seen as the assertion of an ethical self-understanding of the species which is crucial for our capacity to see ourselves as the authors of our own life histories, and to recognize one another as autonomous persons. The attempt to rely on legal means to prevent "liberal eugenics" from becoming normalized, and to ensure the contingency or naturalness of procreation, that is, of the fusion of the parents' sets of chromosomes, would then express something quite different from a vague antimodernistic opposition. Rather, seeking to guarantee the *conditions* under which the practical self-understanding of modernity may be *preserved*, this attempt would itself be a political act of self-referential moral action. This conception, to be sure, is more consistent with the sociological concept of *modernity having become reflective*.[17]

The detraditionalization of lifeworlds is an important aspect of societal modernization; it can be seen as a cognitive adaptation to objective conditions of social life which, as a consequence of the implementation of scientific and technological progress, have time and again been revolutionized. But since the buffers of traditions have, in the course of those processes, been nearly exhausted, modern societies have to rely on their own secular resources for regenerating the energies that ensure their own moral cohesion; that is, on the communicative resources of lifeworlds which have become aware of the immanence of their autopoiesis. From this perspective, the moralizing of "inner nature" rather seems to highlight the "rigidity" of completely modernized lifeworlds which, having lost their backing of metasocial guarantees, are no longer able to respond to new threats to their sociomoral cohesion by new secularizing impulses, let alone by yet another moral and cognitive recasting of religious traditions. Genetic manipulation could change the self-understanding of the species in so fundamental a way that the attack on modern conceptions of law and morality might at the same time affect the inalienable normative foundations of societal integration. Because of this changed form of our *perception* of the processes of modernization, the "moralizing" attempt to adapt biotechnological progress to the by now transparent communicative structures of the lifeworld appears in a different light. Rather than a reenchantment of modernity, this intention now represents the increasing reflexivity of a modernity that realizes its own limits.

This focuses the topic on the question of whether the protection of the integrity of an unmanipulated genetic inheritance can be justified by understanding the biological foundations of personal identity as something not to be disposed of. Legal protection might come to be expressed in a "right to a genetic inheritance immune from artificial intervention." Such a right, which has already been requested by the Parliamentary Assembly of the European Council, would not preempt a ruling on the admissibility of medically based negative eugenics. Such a ruling might still lead, should such be the outcome of moral deliberation and democratic will formation, to restrictions on a fundamental right to unmanipulated hereditary factors.

To narrow down the subject to gene-modifying interventions is to disregard other biopolitical issues. From a liberal perspective, the new reproductive technologies, like substitute organs or medically assisted suicide, are seen as increasing individual autonomy. Critics frequently do not object to the liberal premises, but rather to specific aspects of collaborative procreation, to dubious practices of determining the point of death in view of organ procurement, and to the undesirable social side-effects of having medically assisted suicide determined by law rather than leaving it to professional discretion guided by deontological standards. Other issues which are with good reason controversial are the institutional use of genetic testing and the ways individuals may act on the knowledge provided by predictive diagnostics.

Important bioethical issues like these are certainly connected with the extension of the diagnostic penetration and therapeutic control of human nature. But only with genetic engineering aiming at selection and at the *modification* of traits, as well as with the research required for such goals and geared to future genetic treatment (making it all but impossible to distinguish between basic research and medical use[18]), do challenges of a new order arise.[19] They imply the license to control the physical basis which "we are by nature." What for Kant still belonged to the "kingdom of necessity" had, in the perspective of evolutionary theory, changed to become a "kingdom of contingency." Genetic engineering is now shifting the line between this natural basis we cannot dispose over and the "kingdom of ends." This extension of control of our "inner" nature is distinguished from similar expansions of our scope of options by the fact that it "changes the overall structure of our moral experience."

For Ronald Dworkin, the reason for this is the change of perspective which genetic engineering has brought about for conditions of moral judgment and action that we had previously considered unalterable:

> We distinguish between what nature, including evolution, has created . . . and what we, with the help of these genes, do in this world. In any case, this distinction results in a line being drawn between what we are and the way we deal, on our own account, with this heritage. This decisive line between chance and choice is the backbone of our morality . . . We are afraid of the prospect of human beings designing other human beings, because this option implies shifting the line between chance and choice which is the basis of our value system.[20]

To say that genetic modifications that have as their goal the enhancement of a human life are able to change the overall structure of our moral experience is a strong claim. It can be understood to imply that genetic engineering will confront us, in certain respects, with practical questions concerning some *presuppositions* of moral judgment and action. Shifting the "line between chance and choice" affects the self-understanding of persons who act on moral grounds and are concerned about their life *as a whole*. It makes us aware of the interrelations between our self-understanding as moral beings and the anthropological background of an ethics of the species. Whether or not we may see ourselves as the responsible authors of our own life history and recognize one another as persons of "equal birth", that is of equal dignity, is also dependent on how we see ourselves anthropologically as members of the species. May we consider the genetic self-transformation and self-optimization of the species as a way of increasing the autonomy of the individual? Or will it undermine our normative self-understanding as persons leading their own lives and showing one another equal respect?

If the second alternative is true, we surely don't immediately have a conclusive moral argument, but we do have an orientation relying on an ethics of the species, which urges us to proceed with caution and moderation. But before following this lead, I would like to explain why the detour is necessary. The moral (and controversial constitutional) argument holding that the embryo enjoys full human dignity and is entitled to the absolute protection of its life "from the very beginning" short-circuits the very discussion we cannot bypass if we want, with all the respect we are constitutionally bound to show for the fact of pluralism, to reach a political agreement on these fundamental issues.

II Human dignity versus the dignity of human life

The philosophical dispute[21] over the admissibility of research involving the destruction of embryos and PGD has, to date, followed the path of the debate over abortion. In Germany, this debate has resulted in a regulation stipulating that up to the twelfth week of pregnancy, induced abortion is a fact contrary to law, but one which goes unpunished. If founded on a medical indication considering the welfare of the mother, it is legal. The German population, like that of other countries, is split into two camps over this issue. Insofar as the current discussion is determined by the dispute over abortion, the polarization of "pro-life" versus "pro-choice" advocates has focused attention on the moral status of unborn human life. The conservative side, insisting on the absolute protection of the life of the fertilized embryo, hopes to be able to put a stop to the developments they fear will come out of genetic engineering. But the suggested parallels are misleading. Although the basic normative convictions are the same, they do not at all lead to the same positions in the present case as in the case of abortion. Today, the liberal camp of those holding that women's right to self-determination has precedence over the protection of the life of the embryo in its early stages is split. Those who are guided by deontological intuitions refuse to unconditionally endorse utilitarian statements certifying to the unobjectionability of lifting the ban on the instrumental use of embryos.[22]

Recourse to preimplantation genetic diagnosis, which may prevent potential abortion by allowing genetically deficient extracorporeal stem cells to be "rejected," differs from abortion in relevant aspects. In refusing an unwanted pregnancy, the woman's right to self-determination collides with the embryo's need for protection. In the other case, the conflict is between the protection of the life of the unborn child and a weighing of goods by the parents who, while wanting a child, would abstain from implantation if the embryo is found to be deficient with respect to certain health standards. Moreover, the parents do not find themselves *unexpectedly* propelled into this conflict; by having genetic screening carried out on the embryo, they accept it from the start.

This type of deliberate quality control brings in a new aspect – the instrumentalization of conditionally created human life according to the preferences and value orientations of third parties. Selection is guided by the desired composition of the genome. A decision on existence or nonexistence is taken in view of the potential *essence*. The existential choice of interrupting pregnancy has no more

30

in common with this license to dispose over, or sort out, prenatal life in view of such traits as seem desirable than with the use of prenatal life for research purposes.

Still, in spite of these differences, something can be learned from decades of highly responsible abortion debate. In this controversy, all attempts to describe early human life in terms that are neutral with respect to world-views, that is, not prejudging, and thus acceptable for all citizens of a secular society, have failed.[23] One side will describe the embryo in its early stages of development as a "set of cells" and confront it with the person of the neonate as the first to be accorded human dignity in a strict moral sense. The other side considers the fertilization of the human egg cell to be the relevant beginning of an already individuated, self-regulated evolutionary process. In this perspective, every single specimen of the species that can be *biologically determined* is to be considered a potential person and a subject possessing basic rights. Both sides, it seems, fail to see that something may be "not for us to dispose over" and yet not have the status of a legal person who is a subject of inalienable human rights as defined by the constitution. It does not solely belong to human dignity to qualify as "not to be disposed over" [*"unverfügbar"*]. Something may, for good moral reasons, be not for us to dispose over and still not be "inviolable" [*"unantastbar"*] in the sense of the unrestricted or absolute validity of fundamental rights (which is constitutive for "human dignity" as defined in Article 1 of the Basic Law).

If the dispute over the ascription of "human dignity" as guaranteed by the constitution could be resolved by compelling moral reasons, the deep-rooted anthropological issues of genetic engineering would not extend beyond the ordinary field of moral questions. As it is, the ontological assumptions of a scientistic naturalism, which imply that birth be seen as the relevant caesura, are by no means more trivial or more "scientific" than the metaphysical or religious background assumptions leading to the contrary

31

conclusion. Both sides refer to the fact that *every* attempt to draw a definite line somewhere between fertilization, or the fusion of nuclei, on the one hand, and birth on the other hand is more or less arbitrary because of the high degree of continuity prevailing in the development from organic origins to, first, life capable of feeling and, then, personal life. This continuity thesis, however, seems to me to speak against both attempts to rely on ontological propositions to fix an "absolute" beginning that would also be binding from a normative point of view.

Isn't it still more arbitrary to try to stipulate in favor of one or the other of these sides as a way of coming to an unambiguous moral commitment, resolving the ambivalence of our gradually changing evaluative sentiments and intuitions toward an embryo in the early and middle stages of its development,[24] as compared to a fetus at the later stages, an ambivalence entirely appropriate to the phenomenon concerned? An unambiguous definition of the moral status – be it in terms of Christian metaphysics or of naturalism – is possible only if facts which a pluralistic society is well advised to *leave to controversy* are submitted to a description impregnated by one worldview or another. Nobody doubts the intrinsic value of human life before birth – whether one calls it "sacred" or refuses to sanctify something that is an end in itself. But neither the objectivating language of empiricism nor the language of religion can express the normative substance of the protection to which prepersonal human life is entitled in a way that is rationally acceptable to all citizens.

In the normative disputes of a democratic public, only moral propositions in the strict sense will ultimately count. Only if they are neutral with respect to various worldviews or comprehensive doctrines can propositions on what is equally good for everybody claim to be, for good reasons, acceptable for all. This claim to rational acceptability is the distinguishing mark of propositions for the "just" solution for conflicts of action, as compared to propositions on what, in the context of a life history or in the context of a shared form of life, is "good for me" or "good for us" in the long run. This specific sense of questions of justice will, after all, allow us to come to a conclusion as to the "purpose of morality." This attempt to "define" what morality is all about is, I believe, the appropriate key to finding an answer to the question of how to delimit – irrespective of controversial ontological definitions – the universe of the possible subjects of moral rights and duties.

The community of moral beings creating their own laws refers, in the language of rights and duties, to all matters in need of normative regulation; but only the members of this community can place *one another* under moral obligations and expect *one another* to conform to norms in their behavior. Animals benefit *for their own sake* from the moral duties which we are held to respect in our dealings with sentient creatures. Nevertheless, they do not belong to the universe of members who address intersubjectively accepted rules and orders *to one another*. "Human dignity," as I would like to show, is in a strict moral and legal sense connected with this relational symmetry. It is not a property like intelligence or blue eyes, that one might "possess" by nature; it rather indicates the kind of "inviolability" which comes to have a significance only in interpersonal relations of mutual respect, in the egalitarian dealings among persons. I am not using "inviolability" [*"Unantast-barkeit"*] as a synonym for "not to be disposed over" [*"Unverfügbarkeit"*], because a *postmetaphysical* response to the question of how we should deal with prepersonal human life must not be bought at the price of a *reductionist* definition of humanity and of morality.

I conceive of moral behavior as a constructive response to the dependencies rooted in the incompleteness of our organic makeup and in the persistent frailty (most felt in the phases of childhood, illness, and old age) of our bodily existence. Normative regulation of interpersonal relations may be seen as a porous shell protecting a vulnerable body, and the person incorporated in this body, from the contingencies they are exposed to. Moral rules are fragile constructions protecting *both* the physis from bodily injuries and the person from inner or symbolical injuries. Subjectivity, being what makes the human body a soul-possessing receptacle of the spirit, is itself constituted through intersubjective relations to others. The individual self will only emerge through the course of social externalization, and can only be *stabilized* within the network of undamaged relations of mutual recognition.

This dependency on the other explains why one can be hurt by the other. The person is most exposed to, and least protected from, injuries in the very relations which she is most dependent on for the development of her identity and for the maintenance of her integrity – for example, when giving herself to a partner in an intimate relationship. In its detranscendentalized version, Kant's "free will" no longer descends from the sky as a property of intelligible beings. Autonomy, rather, is a precarious achievement of finite beings who may attain something like "strength," if at all, only if they are mindful of their physical vulnerability and social dependence.[25] If this is the "purpose" of morality, it also explains its "limits." It is the universe of possible interpersonal relations and interactions that is in need as well as capable of moral regulation. Only within this network of legitimately regulated relations of mutual recognition can human beings develop and – together with their physical integrity – maintain a personal identity.

Since man, biologically speaking, is born "unfinished" and subject to lifelong dependency on the help, care, and respect of his social environment, individuation by DNA sequences is revealed as *incomplete* as soon as the process of social individuation sets in.[26] Individuation, as a part of life history, is an outcome of socialization. For the organism to become, with birth, a person in the full sense of this term, an act of social individuation is required, that is, integration in the *public* context of interaction of an intersubjectively shared lifeworld.[27] It is not until the moment the symbiosis with the mother is resolved that the child enters a world of persons who can *approach* it, address it and talk to it. As a member of a species, as a specimen of a community of procreation, the genetically individuated child *in utero* is by no means a fully fledged person "from the very beginning." It takes entrance in the public sphere of a linguistic community for a natural creature to develop into both an individual and a person endowed with reason.[28]

In the symbolical network constituted by the relations of mutual recognition of communicatively acting persons, the neonate is identified as "one of us." He gradually learns to identify himself – simultaneously as a person in general, as a part or a member of his social community (or communities), and as an individual who is unmistakably unique and morally nonexchangeable.[29] This tripartite differentiation of self-reference mirrors the structure of linguistic communication. It is only here, in the space of reasons (Sellars) disclosed through discourse, that the innate faculty of reason can, in the difference of the manifold perspectives of the self and the world, unfold its unifying and consensus-creating force.

Human life, as the point of reference for our obligations, even before its entry into the contexts of public interaction, enjoys legal protection without being itself a subject of either duties or human rights. We must take care not to draw the wrong conclusions from this. Parents do not only talk *about* the child growing in the womb, they *in a certain sense* already communicate *with* it. It does not take the visualization of the unmistakably human features of the fetus shown on the screen to transform the child moving in the womb into an addressee of *anticipatory socialization*. Of course we are under moral and legal obligations toward it *for its own sake*. Moreover, prepersonal life that has not yet reached a stage at which it can be addressed in the *ascribed role* of a second person still has an integral value for an *ethically* constituted form of life as a whole. It is in this respect that we feel compelled to distinguish between the dignity of human life and human dignity as guaranteed by law to every person – a distinction which, incidentally, is also echoed in the phenomenology of our highly emotional attitude toward the dead.

Recent press reports commented on an amendment to the law regulating funeral procedures in the state of Bremen. Referring to stillborn and prematurely born children, this amendment stipulates that due respect toward dead life be shown also when dealing with fetuses. Fetuses, it reads, should no longer be treated as "ethical garbage," as the officialese wording was, but be buried anonymously in collective graves in a cemetery. The very reaction of the reader to the obscene term – let alone the embarrassing practice – betrays, *in the contre-jour* of the dead embryo, the widespread and deep-rooted awe inspired by the integrity of nascent human life no civilized society may unconditionally touch on. On the other hand, the newspaper's comment on the anonymous collective burial also sheds a light on the intuitive distinction I am driving at here: "The Parliament of Bremen was aware of the fact that it would be an unreasonable demand – and perhaps even tantamount to a pathological collective mourning – to have embryos and fetuses buried on the same footing with the postnatal deceased . . . The respect due to a dead human being may well be expressed in different forms of burial."[30]

There is no twilight zone beyond the boundaries of a rigorously defined community of moral persons where we may act irrespective of normative rules and unscrupulously tamper with things. If, on the other hand, the interpretation of morally saturated legal terms like "human right" and "human dignity" tends to be counterintuitively construed in too broad a sense, they will not only lose their power to provide clear conceptual distinctions, but also their critical potential. Violations of human *rights* must not be reduced to the scale of offences against *values*.[31] The difference between rights, which are exempt from weighing, and goods, which can be weighed and ranked accordingly as primary or secondary, should not be blurred.[32]

The nature of the inhibitions we feel in dealing with human life before birth and after death, being hard to define, explains our choice of semantically *broad* terms. Even in its anonymous forms, human life possesses "dignity" and commands "respect." The term of "dignity" comes to mind because it covers a broad semantic range only suggestive of the more specific term of "human dignity." The semantics of "dignity" also include the traces of connotations which are much more obvious, due to the history of its premodern use, in the concept of "honor" – connotations, that is, of an ethos determined by social status. The dignity of the king was embodied in styles of thought and behavior belonging to a form of life entirely different from that of the wife or the bachelor, the workman or the executioner. Abstraction from these concrete manifestations of so many specific dignities became possible only with the advent of "human dignity" as something attached to the person as such. Still, we should not let ourselves be inveigled, by this step of abstraction leading to "human dignity" and – to Kant's single – "human right," into forgetting that the moral community of free and equal subjects of human rights does not form a "kingdom of ends" in the noumenal beyond, but remains embedded in concrete forms of life and their ethos.

III The embedding of morality in an ethics of the species

If morality is situated in a linguistically structured form of life, the current dispute over the admissibility of research involving the destruction of embryos and PGD cannot be resolved by a single argument concluding that the fertilized egg cell possesses, in the strict sense, "human dignity" and has the status of a subject possessing human rights. I indeed understand, and even share, the motive for wanting

37

to use such an argument. A restrictive concept of human dignity implies that the embryo's need for, and entitlement to, protection is subjected to a weighing of goods which would leave the door open a crack for an instrumentalization of human life and for the erosion of the categorical sense of moral inhibitions. It is, therefore, all the more important to search for a solution which is at once conclusive and neutral with respect to competing worldviews, a neutrality we are anyway committed to by the constitutional principle of tolerance. Even if my own understanding, as proposed here, of the purpose as well as the limit of morality should fail to meet this claim and be found guilty of a metaphysical bias, the consequence would still be the same. If it is democratically constituted and committed to inclusion, the neutral state must refrain from taking sides in an "ethically" controversial reference to Articles 1 and 2 of the German constitution. If the question of how to deal with unborn human life is an ethical one, there is every reason to expect well-founded dissent to arise, as was the case in the debate of the Bundestag on May 31. The philosophical debate, disburdened of sterile polarizations, may then focus on the issue of an appropriate ethical self-understanding of the species.

First, however, a note on linguistic usage. I call "moral" such issues as deal with the just way of living together. Actors who may come into conflict with one another address these issues when they are confronted with social interactions in need of normative regulation. Conflicts of this type may be reasonably expected to be in principle amenable to rational solutions that are in the equal interest of all. No such rational acceptability may be expected, by contrast, if the description of the conflictual situation as well as the justification of pertinent norms are themselves shaped by the preferred way of life and the existential self-understanding of an individual or a group of citizens, that is, by their identity-forming beliefs. Background conflicts of this kind touch upon "ethical" issues.

Persons and communities whose existence may go wrong address questions of a happy or not misspent life with regard to values that direct their life history or form of life. Such ethical questions are tailored to the perspective of persons who, within the context of their life, want to understand who they are and which practices are, on the whole, best for them. Nations differ in their attitudes towards the mass crimes of former regimes. Strategies of forgiving and forgetting or processes of punishment and critical reappraisal will be chosen in accordance with their historical experience and collective self-understanding. Their attitude toward nuclear energy will depend, among other things, on their ranking of security and health as compared to economic prosperity. For ethical-political questions like these, it is "so many cultures, so many customs."

The questions raised, in contrast, by our attitude toward prepersonal human life are of an altogether different caliber. They do not touch on this or that difference in the great variety of cultural forms of life, but on those intuitive self-descriptions that guide our own identification *as human beings* – that is, our self-understanding as members of the species. They concern not culture, which is different everywhere, but the vision different cultures have of "man" who – in his anthropological universality – is everywhere the same. If I am not mistaken in my assessment of the debate over the "use" of embryos for research, or over the conditional creation of embryos, it is disgust at something obscene rather than moral indignation proper that comes to be expressed in our emotional reactions. It is the feeling of vertigo that seizes us when the ground beneath our feet, which we believed to be solid, begins to slip. Symptomatically, it is revulsion we feel when confronted with the chimaera that bear witness to a violation of the species boundaries that we had naively assumed to be unalterable. This "ethical virgin soil," rightly termed such by Otfried Höffe,[33] consists of the very uncertainty that invades the identity of the species. The perceived, and dreaded, advances of genetic engineering affect the very concept we have of ourselves as cultural members of the species of "humanity" – to which there seems to be no alternative.

Of course, these ideas also are plural. Cultural forms of life are bound up with systems of interpretations that explain the position of humanity in the universe and provide the "thick" anthropological context in which the prevailing moral code is embedded. In pluralistic societies, these metaphysical or religious interpretations of the self and the world are, for good reasons, subordinated to the moral foundations of the constitutional state, which is neutral with respect to competing worldviews and committed to their peaceful coexistence. Under the condition of postmetaphysical thought, the ethical self-understanding of the species, which is inscribed in specific traditions and forms of life, no longer provides the arguments for overruling the claims of a morality presumed to be universally accepted. But this "priority of the just over the good" must not blind us to the fact that the abstract morality of reason proper to subjects of human rights is itself sustained by a prior *ethical self-understanding of the species*, which is shared by all *moral persons*.

Like the great world religions, metaphysical doctrines and humanistic traditions also provide contexts in which the "overall structure of our moral experience" is embedded. They express, in one way or the other, an anthropological self-understanding of the species that is consistent with an autonomous morality. The religious interpretations of the self and the world that were elaborated by highly advanced civilizations during the axial age converge, so to speak, in a minimal ethical self-understanding of the species sustaining this kind of morality. As long as the one and the other are in harmony, the priority of the just over the good is not problematical.

This perspective inevitably gives rise to the question of whether the instrumentalization of human nature changes the ethical self-understanding of the species in such a way that we may no longer see ourselves as ethically free and morally equal beings guided by norms and reasons. For the self-evident nature of elementary background assumptions to crumble, it takes the unanticipated emergence of surprising alternatives (even though these novel facts – like the artificial "chimaera" of transgenic organisms – have their archaic prefigurations in mythical images). Irritants of this kind are provoked by all the current scenarios that step out of science-fiction literature and invade the scientific feature pages. Thus we are of late confronted, by a strange lot of non-fiction authors, with the vision of humans being improved by chip implants, or ousted by intelligent robots.

To illustrate the technologically assisted life-processes of the human organism, nano-engineers draw up visions of man and machine fused into a production plant subjected to autoregulated processes of supervision and renewal, permanent repair and upgrading. In this vision, self-replicating microrobots circulate in the human body, combining with organic matter in order, for instance, to stop ageing processes or to boost the functions of the cerebrum. Computer engineers, as well, have not been idle, contributing to this genre by drawing up the vision of future robots having become autonomous and evolving into machines which mark flesh-and-blood human beings as a model doomed to extinction. These superior intelligences are supposed to have overcome the flaws of human hardware. As to the software, which is modeled on our brains, they promise not only immortality, but unlimited perfection.

Bodies stuffed with prostheses to boost performance, or the intelligence of angels available on hard drives, are fantastic images. They dissolve boundaries and break connections that in our everyday actions have up to now seemed to be of an almost transcendental necessity. There is fusion of the organically grown with the technologically made, on the one hand, and separation of the productivity of the human mind from live subjectivity, on the other hand.

Whether these speculations are manifestations of a fever-ish imagination or serious predictions, an expression of displaced eschatological needs or a new variety of science-fiction science, I refer to them only as examples of an instrumentalization of human nature initiating a change in the ethical self-understanding of the species – a self-understanding no longer consistent with the normative self-understanding of persons who live in the mode of self-determination and responsible action.

The provocation inherent in the advances of genetic engineering that have already been realized or are realis-tically to be expected does as yet not go that far. Still, there is no denying certain analogies.[34] The manipulation of the makeup of the human genome, which is progressively being decoded, and the hopes entertained by certain scientists of soon being able to take evolution in their own hands do, after all, uproot the categorical distinction between the subjective and the objective, the naturally grown and the made, as they extend to regions which, up to now, we could not dispose over. What is at stake is a dedifferentiation, through biotechnology, of deep-rooted categorical distinctions which we have as yet, in the description we give of ourselves, assumed to be invariant. This dedifferentiation might change our ethical self-understanding as a species in a way that could also affect our moral consciousness – the conditions, that is, of nature-like growth which alone allow us to conceive of ourselves as the authors of our own lives and as equal members of the moral community. Knowledge of one's own genome being programmed might prove to be dis-ruptive, I suspect, for our assumption that we exist as a body or, so to speak, "are" our body, and thus may give rise to a novel, curiously asymmetrical type of relationship between persons.

Where have our reflections so far taken us? On the one hand, we cannot, from the premise of pluralism, ascribe to the embryo "from the very beginning" the absolute pro-tection of life enjoyed by persons who are subjects possessing basic rights. On the other hand, there is the intuition that prepersonal human life must not simply be declared free to be included in the familiar balancing of competing goods. To clarify this intuition, I choose to approach it indirectly, via the – at present purely theoretical – possibility of liberal eugenics, which, in the United States, for example, is already being discussed in some detail. In this anticipatory perspective, the contours of the ongoing controversy about the two current issues will emerge more clearly.

Normative restrictions in dealing with embryonic life cannot be directed against genetic interventions as such. The problem, of course, is not genetic engineering, but the mode and scope of its use. It is, moreover, the *attitude* in which interventions in the genetic makeup of potential members of our moral community are carried out that provides the standards for an assessment of their moral admissibility. Thus, in the case of *therapeutic* gene manipulations, we approach the embryo as the second person he will one day be.[35] This clinical attitude draws its legitimizing force from the well-founded counterfactual assumption of a possible consensus reached with another person who is capable of saying yes or no. The burden of normative proof is thus shifted to the justification of an anticipated consent that at present cannot be sought. In the case of a therapeutic intervention in the embryo it might, in the best of cases, be confirmed later (and, in the case of birth being precluded as a preventive act, not at all). What this requirement may really mean in the context of a practice that – like PGD and embryonic research – is only hypothetically, or not at all, aimed at later birth, is still unclear.

In any case, *assumed* consensus can only be invoked for the goal of avoiding evils which are unquestionably extreme and likely to be rejected by all. Thus, the moral community which in the profane realm of everyday politics takes on the sober form of democratically constituted nations must eventually believe itself capable of working out, time and again, from the spontaneous proceedings of everyday living, sufficiently convincing criteria for what is to be understood as a sick, or a healthy, bodily existence. Our commitment to the "logic of healing" is based, I would like to show, on the moral point of view that obliges us, in our dealings with second persons, to refrain from instrumentalizing them and, instead, saddles us – in contrast to the extensive scope left to tolerance by liberal eugenicists – with the responsibility of drawing a line between negative eugenics and enhancing eugenics. The program of liberal eugenics blinds itself to this task because it ignores the biotechnological dedifferentiation of the modes of action.

IV The grown and the made

Our lifeworld is, in a sense, "Aristotelian" in its constitution. In everyday living, we don't think twice before distinguishing between inorganic and organic nature, plants and animals and, again, animal nature and the reasoning and social nature of man. The fact that these categorical divisions are so persistent, even though they are no longer connected with ontological claims, can be explained by referring to perspectives that are closely interlaced with certain modes of dealing with the world. Here again, analysis may proceed along the lines provided by basic Aristotelian principles. Aristotle contrasts the *theoretical* attitude of the disinterested observer of nature with two other attitudes. He distinguishes it, on the one hand, from the *technical* attitude of the actor who is engaged in production and, generally, in purposeful action and who intervenes in nature by employing means and consuming materials. On the other hand, he distinguishes it from the practical attitude of persons who either act with prudence or with an ethical orientation and approach one another in a context of interaction – be it in the objectivating attitude of a strategist anticipating and assessing the decisions

44

his counterparts will make in light of his own preferences, or in the performative attitude of a subject engaged in communicative action who wants to reach an understanding with a second person in the context of an intersubjectively shared world. Still other attitudes are required for the practices of the peasant who tends his cattle and cultivates his soil, or of the doctor who diagnoses diseases in order to heal them, or of the breeder who selects and improves hereditary traits of a population for his own ends. All these classical practices of cultivating, healing, and breeding share a respect for the inherent dynamics of autoregulated nature. If they are not to fail, the cultivating, therapeutic, or selecting interventions have to abide by these dynamics.

The "logic" of these forms of action which, in Aristotle, were still tailored to corresponding regions of being, has lost the ontological dignity of opening up specific perspectives on the world. In this dedifferentiation, modern experimental sciences played an important role. They combined the objectivating attitude of the disinterested observer with the technical attitude of an intervening actor producing experimental effects. The cosmos was no longer perceived as an object of pure contemplation; and "soulless" nature, as seen by nominalism, was subjected to a different kind of objectivation. This gearing of science to the task of converting an objectivated nature into something we may control by technological means had an important impact on the process of societal modernization. In the course of their redefinition by science, most fields of practice were impregnated and restructured by the "logic" of the application of scientific technologies.

This adjustment of the societal modes of production and interaction to the advances of science and technology certainly caused the imperatives of a single form of action, the instrumental one, to become predominant. Nevertheless, the architecture of the modes of action has itself remained intact. To the present day, morality and law still function as the normative controls for practical life in complex societies. It is true that, just like the mechanization of agriculture, which was rationalized according to business management principles, the technological equipment and upgrading of a health-care system dependent on pharmaceutical businesses and medical machinery have been prone to crises. But these crises have acted as a reminder of the logic of medical action or of ecological ways of dealing with nature rather than made them disappear. The decrease in social relevance of the "clinical" modes of action in the broadest sense has been counterbalanced by an increase in their legitimacy. Today, genetic research and the advances of genetic engineering are justified by referring to biopolitical goals of improved nutrition, health, and a prolonged lifespan. We therefore tend to forget that the revolution of breeding practices by genetic engineering is itself no longer governed by the clinical mode of *adjustment* to the inherent dynamic of nature. What it suggests, rather, is the *dedifferentiation* of a fundamental distinction which is also constitutive of our self-understanding as species members.

To the degree that the evolution of the species, proceeding by random selection, comes within the reach of the interventions of genetic engineering and, thus, of actions we have to answer for, the categories of what is *manufactured* and what has *come to be by nature*, which in the lifeworld still retain their demarcating power, dedifferentiate. For us, this distinction is self-evident because it refers to familiar modes of action: the technical use made of matter, on the one hand, and the cultivating or therapeutic attitude toward organic nature, on the other hand. The care we take when we deal with self-maintaining systems, whose self-regulation we might disrupt, bears witness not only to a *cognitive* consideration for the inherent dynamic of the process of life. The closer we are to the species dealt with, the more clearly this consideration is intermingled also with a *practical* concern, a kind of respect. The empathy, or "resonant comprehension," we show for the violability of organic life, acting as a check upon our practical dealings, is obviously grounded in the sensitivity of our own body and in the distinction we make between any kind of subjectivity, however rudimentary, and the world of objects which can merely be manipulated.

Biotechnological intervention, in replacing clinical treatment, intercepts this "correspondence" with other living beings. The biotechnological mode of action, however, differs from the technical intervention of the engineer by a relation of "collaboration" – or "tinkering around"[36] – with the nature we thus dispose over:

> In dealing with dead matter, the producer, confronted with a passive material, is the only one to act. In dealing with organisms, activity is confronted with activity: biotechnology is collaborative with the auto-activity of active material, the biological system in its natural functioning into which a new determinant has to be incorporated . . . The mode of the technological act is intervention, not building.[37]

From this description, Hans Jonas goes on to infer the specific self-referentiality and irreversibility of intervention in a complex, self-regulated process, leading to consequences which we cannot control: "To 'produce,' here, means to commit something to the stream of evolution in which the producer himself is carried along."[38]

Now, the more ruthless the intrusion into the makeup of the *human* genome becomes, the more inextricably the clinical mode of treatment is assimilated to the biotechnological mode of intervention, blurring the intuitive distinction between the grown and the made, the subjective and the objective – with repercussions reaching as far as the self-reference of the person to her bodily existence. The vanishing point of this development is characterized by Jonas as follows: "Technologically mastered nature now again includes man who (up to now) had, in technology, set himself against it as its master." With the genetic pro-

47

gramming of human beings, domination of nature turns into an act of self-empowering of man, thus changing our self-understanding as members of the species – and *perhaps* touching upon a necessary condition for an autonomous conduct of life and a universalistic understanding of morality. Hans Jonas addresses this concern by asking: "But whose power is this – and over whom or over what? Obviously the power of those living today over those coming after them, who will be the defenseless objects of prior choices made by the planners of today. The other side of the power of today is the future bondage of the living to the dead."

By bringing the issue to this dramatic point, Jonas resituates genetic engineering in the context of a self-destructive dialectics of enlightenment, according to which the species itself reverts from domination of nature to servitude to nature.[39] The "species" as a collective singular is also the point of reference for a debate between a teleology of nature and a philosophy of history, between Jonas and Spaemann on the one hand, Horkheimer and Adorno on the other hand. This debate, however, takes place on too high a level of abstraction. What we need to do is to come to a clear distinction between the authoritarian and the liberal varieties of eugenics. Biopolitics is, as yet, not guided by the goal of an enhancement, however defined, of the gene pool of the species as a whole. The moral reasons that prohibit individual persons from being taken as mere exemplars of the species, and instrumentalized for such a collectivist goal, are still solidly rooted in the principles that underlie our constitution and law.

In liberal societies, eugenic decisions would be transferred, via markets governed by profit orientation and preferential demands, to the individual choice of parents and, on the whole, to the anarchic whims of consumers and clients:

> While old-fashioned authoritarian eugenicists sought to produce citizens out of a single centrally designed mould,

the distinguishing mark of the new liberal eugenics is state neutrality. Access to information about the full range of genetic therapies will allow prospective parents to look to their own values in selecting improvements for future children. Authoritarian eugenicists would do away with ordinary procreative freedoms. Liberals instead propose radical extension of them.[40]

This program, however, is compatible with political liberalism only if enhancing genetic interventions neither limit the opportunities to lead an autonomous life for the person genetically treated, nor constrain the conditions for her to interact with other persons on an egalitarian basis.

In order to justify the normative admissibility of these interventions, advocates of liberal eugenics compare the genetic modification of hereditary factors to the modification of attitudes and expectations taking place in the course of socialization. They want to show that, from the moral point of view, there is no great difference between eugenics and education: "If special tutors and camps, training programs, even the administration of growth hormones to add a few inches in height are within parental rearing discretion, why should genetic intervention to enhance normal offspring traits be any less legitimate?"[41] This argument is supposed to justify the inclusion of the parents' eugenic freedom to improve the genetic makeup of their children in the scope of parental discretion which is guaranteed anyway. The parents' eugenic freedom, however, is subject to the reservation that it must not enter into collision with the ethical freedom of their children. Advocates reassure themselves by pointing out that genetic dispositions always interact with the environment in a contingent way and are not transposed, in linear fashion, into features of the phenotype. Therefore, they say, genetic programming is no inadmissible intrusion upon the future life-projects of the programmed person:

> The liberal linkage of eugenic freedom with parental discretion in respect of educationally or dietarily assisted

improvement makes sense in the light of this modern understanding. If gene and environment are of parallel importance in accounting for the traits we currently possess, attempts to modify people by modifying either of them would seem to deserve similar scrutiny . . . We should think of both types of modification in similar ways.[42]

The argument rests entirely on a dubious parallel, which itself presupposes a leveling out of the difference between the grown and the made, the subjective and the objective.

As we saw, manipulation extending to the hereditary factors of humans rescinds the distinction between clinical action and technical fabrication with respect to our own inner nature. Someone who performs treatment on an embryo approaches the quasi-subjective nature of this embryo in the same perspective as he would approach objective nature. This perspective suggests that acting on the composition of a human genome does not essentially differ from acting on the environment of a person growing up: her own nature is ascribed to this person as constituting an "inner environment." But isn't there a collision between this ascription, which is carried out from the perspective of the intervening person, and the self-perception of the person concerned?

A person "has" or "possesses" her body only through "being" this body in proceeding with her life. It is from this phenomenon of being a body and, at the same time, having a body [Leibsein und Körperhaben] that Helmut Plessner set out to describe and analyze the "excentric position" of man.[43] Cognitive developmental psychology has shown that having a body is the result of the capacity of assuming an objectivating attitude toward the prior fact of being a body, a capacity we do not acquire until youth. The primary mode of experience, and also the one "by" which the subjectivity of the human person lives, is that of being a body.[44]

To the extent that his body is revealed to the adolescent who was eugenically manipulated as something which is also made, the participant perspective of the actual experience of living one's own life collides with the reifying perspective of a producer or a bricoleur. The parents' choice of a genetic program for their child is associated with intentions which later take on the form of expectations addressed to the child, without, however, providing the addressee with an opportunity to take a *revisionist* stand. The programming intentions of parents who are ambitious and given to experimentation, or of parents who are merely concerned, have the peculiar status of a one-sided and unchallengeable expectation. In the life history of the person concerned, the transformed expectations turn up as a normal element of interactions, and yet elude the conditions of reciprocity required for communication proper. In making their choice, the parents were only looking to their own preferences, as if disposing over an object. But since the object evolves to be a person, the egocentric intervention takes on the meaning of a communicative action which *might* have existential consequences for the adolescent. But genetically fixed "demands" cannot, strictly speaking, be responded to. In their role as programmers, the parents are barred from entering the dimension of the life history where they might confront their child as the authors of demands they address to him. Liberal eugenicists, in likening fate dependent on nature to fate resulting from socialization, have settled for too easy a solution.

The assimilation of clinical action to manipulating intervention also makes it easy for them to take the next step of leveling out the substantial distinction between negative and positive eugenics. Highly generalized goals, for instance strengthening the immunosystem or prolonging the lifespan, are of course positive and, nevertheless, consistent with clinical goals. However hard it may be to distinguish in the individual case between therapeutic interventions – the prevention of evils – and enhancing interventions, the regulative idea that governs the intended delimitation is simple.[45] As long as medical intervention is guided by the clinical goal of healing a disease or of making provisions for a healthy life, the person carrying out the treatment may assume that he has the consent of the patient preventively treated.[46] The presumption of informed consent transforms egocentric action into communicative action. As long as the geneticist intervening in a human being conceives of himself as a doctor, there is no need for him to approach the embryo in the objectivating attitude of the technician, that is, as an object which is manufactured or repaired or channeled into a desired direction. He may, in the performative attitude of a participant in interaction, anticipate the future person's consent to an essentially contestable goal of the treatment. I would like to stress the point that what solely matters here is not the ontological status of the embryo, but the clinical attitude of the first person toward another person – however virtual – who, some time in the future, may encounter him in the role of a second person.

A preventively "healed" patient may later, as a person, assume a different attitude toward this type of prenatal intervention than someone who learns that his genetic makeup was programmed without his virtual consent, so to speak, according to the sole preferences of a third person. Only in the latter case does genetic intervention take on the form of an instrumentalization of human nature. In contrast to clinical intervention, the genetic material is, in this case, manipulated from the perspective of a person engaging in instrumental action in order to "collaboratively" induce, in the realm of objects, a state that is desirable according to her own goals. Genetic interventions involving the manipulation of traits constitute positive eugenics if they cross the line defined by the logic of healing, that is, the prevention of evils which one may assume to be subject to general consent.

Liberal eugenics needs to face the question of whether the *perceived* dedifferentiation of the grown and the made, the subjective and the objective, is likely to affect the autonomous conduct of life and moral self-understanding of the programmed person. In any case, normative evaluation is not possible unless we ourselves adopt the perspective of the persons concerned.

V Natality, the capacity of being oneself, and the ban on instrumentalization

What is so disconcerting for our moral feelings in the idea of eugenic programming is succinctly and soberly put by Andreas Kuhlmann: "Of course, parents have always been given to wishful thinking as to what is going to become of their offspring. Still, this is different from children being confronted with prefabricated visions which, all in all, they owe their existence to."[47] To associate this intuition with genetic determinism would be to misconstrue it.[48] Irrespective of how far genetic programming could actually go in fixing properties, dispositions, and skills, as well as in determining the behavior of the future person, *post factum* knowledge of this circumstance may intervene in the self-relation of the person, the relation to her bodily or mental existence. The change would take place in the mind. Awareness would shift, as a consequence of this change of perspective, from the performative attitude of a first person living her own life to the observer perspective which governed the intervention one's own body was subjected to before birth. When the adolescent learns about the design drawn up by another person for intervening in her genetic features in order to modify certain traits, the perspective of being a grown body may be superseded – in her objectivating self-perception – by the perspective of being something made. In this way, the dedifferentiation of the distinction between the grown and the made intrudes upon one's subjective mode of existence. It might usher in the vertiginous awareness that, as a consequence of a genetic intervention carried out before we were born, the subjective nature we experience as being something we cannot dispose over is actually the result of an instru-

53

mentalization of a part of our nature. The realization that our hereditary factors were, in a past before our past, subjected to programming, confronts us on an existential level, so to speak, with the expectation that we subordinate our being a body to our having a body.

We should, however, remain skeptical about this imaginary dramatization of anticipated facts. Who knows, after all, whether knowledge of the fact that the makeup of my genome was designed by someone else need be of any significance at all for my life? It is rather unlikely that the perspective of being a body will lose its primacy over that of having a genetically tailored body. The participating perspective implied in the experience of being a body can only intermittently be *transposed* to the external perspective of a (self-)observer. Knowledge of the temporal *prius* of being made does not necessarily result in self-alienation. Why should people not get used to this, too, and shrug it off by saying "so what?"? Why shouldn't we, after the narcissistic insult suffered through the disruption of our geocentric and our anthropocentric worldviews by Copernicus and Darwin, respectively, approach this third decentration of our worldview – the subjugation of our body and our life to biotechnology – with more composure?

A human being who has been eugenically programmed has to live with the awareness that his hereditary features were manipulated in order to act purposefully on his phenotypic molding. But before coming to a conclusion as to the normative assessment of this possibility, we have to clarify the standards by which such an instrumentalization might be judged a transgression. Moral convictions and norms are, as I said, situated in forms of life which are reproduced through the members' communicative actions. Since individuation is achieved through the socializing medium of thick linguistic communication, the integrity of individuals is particularly dependent on the respect underlying their dealings with one another. This, in any case, is how we may understand the first two phras-

54

ings Kant gives of the moral principle. The "formula of ends" of the categorical imperative expresses the claim that every person is to be regarded "always at the same time as an end in himself" and "never" to be treated "simply as a means." Even in cases of conflict, the persons involved are to go on interacting in an attitude of communicative action. They are to attune themselves, from the participant perspective of a first person, to the other as a second person, with the intention of reaching an understanding with him instead of reifying and instrumentalizing him, in the observer perspective of a third person, for their own ends. The morally relevant limit to instrumentalization is set by what, in the second person, will be out of my reach as long as the communicative relationship, that is, the possibility of assuming a yes- or no-position remains unimpaired. The limit is set by the very things with which and by which a person is himself in acting and in standing up to critics. The "self" of this end in itself we are obliged to respect in the other person is primarily expressed in the authorship of a life guided by his own aspirations. Everybody interprets the world from his point of view, acts according to his own motives, is the source of authentic aspirations.

It is not sufficient, however, for the acting subjects to conform to the ban on instrumentalization by monitoring (in Harry Frankfurt's sense) their choice of primary ends in the light of their own higher ends; that is, generalized goals or values. The categorical imperative requires every single person to give up the perspective of a first person in order to join an intersubjectively shared "we"-perspective which enables all of them together to attain value orientations *which can be generalized*. Kant's "formula of ends" already provides the bridge to the "formula of laws". The idea that a valid norm must be of a kind that can be generally accepted is suggested by the remarkable provision enjoining us to respect "humanity" in every single person by treating her as an end in itself: "Act in such a way that you always treat humanity, whether in your own person or in the person of any other, never simply as a means, but always at the same time as an end." The concept of humanity obliges us to take up the "we"-perspective from which we perceive one another as members of an *inclusive* community no person is excluded from.

The way in which normative agreement may be reached in cases of conflict is then expressed by the other formula of the categorical imperative, which enjoins us to subject our own will to the very maxims which everybody may want to see as a universal law. It follows from this that, every time a dissensus over underlying value orientations arises, subjects who act autonomously must engage in discourse in a joint effort to discover or to work out the norms which in view of a matter in need of regulation *deserve* the well-founded consent of all. Both phrasings explain the same intuition from a different angle. On the one hand, there is the nature of the person "being an end in itself" who as an inexchangeable individual is supposed to be capable of leading a life of his own; on the other hand, there is the equal respect which every person in his quality as a person is entitled to. Therefore, the universality of moral norms ensuring equal treatment for all cannot be an abstract one; it has to be sensitive to the individual situations and life-projects of every single person.

This is accounted for by a concept of morality where individuation and generalization interpenetrate. The authority of the first person, as expressed in specific experiences, authentic aspirations, and the initiative for responsible actions, that is, all in all, in the authorship for one's own life conduct, must not be violated even by the self-legislation of the moral community. Morality will ensure the freedom of the individual to lead his own life only if the application of generalized norms does not unreasonably lace in the scope for choosing and developing one's life-project. In the very universality of valid norms, a nonassimilative, noncoercive intersubjective communality gets expressed in view of the whole range of a reasonable variety of interests and interpretive perspectives, neither

leveling out nor suppressing nor marginalizing nor exclud-
ing the voices of the others – the strangers, the dissidents,
and the powerless.

Such are the requirements which must be met by the
rationally motivated consent of independent subjects
who are capable of saying no. Any agreement reached by
rational discourse relies for its validity on the double nega-
tion of objections that were rejected for good reasons. But
the only way for this agreement reached through practical discourse to avoid being an *overpowering* consensus is
to integrate the entire complexity of the objections
reasonably refuted as well as the unrestricted variety of
interests and interpretive perspectives that were *taken into
account*. For the person expressing a moral judgment,
therefore, her own capacity of being herself is as important as is the fact for the person engaging in moral action
that the other is being herself. In the yes or no of participants in discourse, the spontaneous self- and world-
understanding of individuals *who are irreplaceable* must
find its appropriate expression.

What is true for action is true for discourse: Her yes and
no counts because and inasmuch as it is the person *herself*
who is behind her intentions, initiatives, and aspirations. If
we see ourselves as moral persons, we intuitively assume
that since we are inexchangeable, we act and judge *in
propria persona* – that it is our own voice speaking and no
other. It is for this "capacity of being oneself" that the "intention of another person" intruding upon our life history
through the genetic program might primarily turn out to
be disruptive. The capacity of being oneself requires that
the person be at home, so to speak, in her own body. The
body is the medium for incarnating the personal mode of
existence in such a way that any kind of self-reference, as
for instance first person sentences, is not only unnecessary,
but meaningless.[49] It is the body that our sense of direction
refers to, denoting center and periphery, the own and the
alien. It is the person's incarnation in the body that not only
enables us to distinguish between active and passive,

57

causing to happen and happening, making and finding; it also compels us to differentiate between actions we ascribe to ourselves and actions we ascribe to others. But bodily existence enables the person to distinguish between these perspectives only on condition that she identifies with her body. And for the person to feel one with her body, it seems that this body has to be experienced as something natural – as a continuation of the organic, self-regenerative life from which the person was born.

We experience our own freedom with reference to something which, by its very nature, is not at our disposal. The person, irrespective of her finiteness, knows herself to be the irreducible origin of her own actions and aspirations. But in order to know this, is it really necessary for this person to be able to ascribe her own origin to a beginning which eludes human disposal, to a beginning, that is, which is sure not to prejudge her freedom only if it may be seen as something – like God or nature – that is not at the disposal of some *other* person? Birth as well, being a natural fact, meets the conceptual requirement of constituting a beginning we cannot control. Philosophy has but rarely addressed this matter. One of the exceptions is Hannah Arendt, who in the context of her theory of action introduces the concept of "natality."

She starts out from the observation that each time a child is born, it is not only another life history which begins, but a new one. She then connects this emphatic beginning of human life with the self-understanding of acting subjects as being able, of their own free will, to "make a new beginning." For Arendt, every single birth, being invested with the hope for something entirely other to come and break the chain of eternal recurrence, is to be seen in the eschatological light of the biblical promise: "a child has been born unto us." The "expectation of the unexpected" is betrayed by the emotion in the eyes of the curious bystanders who witness the arrival of the newborn child. On this indeterminate hope of something new, the power of the past over the future is shattered. For Arendt, the concept of natality is the bridge which connects the natural beginning with the awareness of the adult subject:

> the new beginning inherent in birth can make itself felt in the world only because the newcomer possesses the capacity of beginning something anew, that is, of acting. In this sense of initiative, an element of action, and therefore of natality, is inherent in all human activities. Moreover, since action is the political activity par excellence, natality, and not mortality, may be the central category of political, as distinguished from metaphysical, thought.[50]

In acting, human beings feel free to begin something new because birth itself, as a divide between nature and culture, marks a new beginning.[51] What is suggested by this is, I believe, the onset, with birth, of a differentiation between the socialization fate of a person and the natural fate of her organism. It is only by referring to this difference between nature and culture, between beginnings not at our disposal, and the plasticity of historical practices that the acting subject may proceed to the self-ascriptions without which he could not perceive himself as the initiator of his actions and aspirations. For a person to be himself, a point of reference is required which goes back beyond the lines of tradition and the contexts of interaction which constitute the process of formation through which personal identity is molded in the course of a life history.

Of course, the person can only see himself as the author of ascribable actions and as the source of authentic aspirations if he assumes continuity for a self, remaining self-identical in the course of a life history. Failing this assumption, we would be capable neither of assuming a reflective attitude toward our socialization fate, nor of developing a revisionary self-understanding. The actual awareness of being the author of one's actions and aspirations is interwoven with the intuition that we are called upon to be the authors of a critically appropriated life history. A person, however, who would be the sole product of a suffered socialization fate would see his "self" slip away in the stream of constellations, relations, and relevancies imposed upon the formation process. We can achieve continuity in the vicissitudes of a life history only because we may refer, for establishing the difference between what *we* are and what happens *to us*, to a bodily existence which is itself the continuation of a natural fate going back beyond the socialization process. The fact that this natural fate, this past before our past, so to speak, is not at our human disposal seems to be essential for our awareness of freedom – but is it also essential for the capacity, as such, of being oneself?

From Hannah Arendt's suggestive description, it does not actually follow that the anonymous chains of action cutting across the genetically manipulated body will necessarily lead to this body losing its worth, the basis on which to ascribe the feeling of being oneself. Are we to suppose, once a discernable intrusion of the intentions of third persons upon a genetic program has occurred, that birth no longer constitutes a beginning that could give the acting subject an awareness of being able to make a new beginning, any time? Of course, being confronted with the sedimented intention of a third person in one's hereditary factors requires the subject concerned to come to terms with this fact. The programmed person cannot see the programmer's intention, reaching through the genome, as a contingent circumstance restricting her scope of action. With his intention, the programmer rather intervenes as a co-player in an interaction without turning up as an opponent *within* the field of action of the programmed person. But what, in this peculiar unassailability of another *peer's* intention is questionable in a moral sense?

VI The moral limits of eugenics

In liberal societies, every citizen has an equal right to pursue his individual life projects "as best he can." This ethical scope of the freedom to make the best of a life which may go wrong is *also* determined by genetically conditioned abilities, dispositions, and properties. With regard to the ethical freedom to lead a life of one's own while being subject to organic conditions not of our own choice, the situation of the programmed person does not initially differ from that of a person naturally begotten. Eugenic programming of desirable traits and dispositions, however, gives rise to moral misgivings as soon as it commits the person concerned to a specific life-project or, in any case, puts specific restrictions on his freedom to choose a life of his own. Of course, the adolescent may assimilate the "alien" intention which caring parents long before his birth associated with the disposition to certain skills much in the same way as might be the case, for instance, for certain vocational traditions running in a family. For the adolescent confronted with the expectations of ambitious parents to make something out of, for instance, his mathematical or musical talents, it makes no fundamental difference whether this confrontation takes place in terms of the dense fabric of domestic socialization, or in dealing with a genetic program, provided he appropriates these expectations as aspirations of his own and sees the indicated talents as an opportunity as well as an obligation to engage in efforts of his own.

If an intention is "appropriated" in this way, no effect of alienation from one's own existence as a body and a soul will occur, nor will the corresponding restrictions of the ethical freedom to live a life of one's own be felt. On the other hand, as long as we cannot be sure that this harmony between one's own intentions and those of a third party will inevitably be produced, we cannot rule out the possibility of *dissonant* cases. Cases of dissonant intentions illuminate the fact that natural fate and socialization fate differ in a morally relevant aspect.[52] Socialization processes proceed only by communicative action, wielding their formative power in the medium of propositional attitudes and decisions which, for the adult persons to

61

whom the child relates, are connected with internal reasons even if, at a given stage of its cognitive development, the "space of reasons" is not yet widely open to the child itself. Due to the interactive structure of the formation processes in which the child always has the role of a second person, expectations underlying the parents' efforts at character building are essentially "contestable." Since even a psychically binding "delegation" of children can only be brought about in the medium of reasons, the adolescents in principle still have the opportunity to respond to and retroactively break away from it.[53] They can retrospectively compensate for the asymmetry of filial dependency by liberating themselves through a critical reappraisal of the genesis of such restrictive socialization processes. Even neurotic fixations may be resolved analytically, through an elaboration of self-reflexive insights.

But in the case of a genetic determination carried out according to the parents' own preferences, there is no such opportunity. With genetic enhancement, there is no communicative scope for the projected child to be addressed as a second person and to be involved in a communication process. From the adolescent's perspective, an instrumental determination cannot, like a pathogenic socialization process, be revised by "critical reappraisal." It does not permit the adolescent looking back on the prenatal intervention to engage in a *revisionary* learning process. *Being at odds with* the genetically fixed intention of a third person is hopeless. The genetic program is a mute and, in a sense, unanswerable fact; for unlike persons born naturally, someone who is at odds with genetically fixed intentions is barred from developing, in the course of a reflectively appropriated and deliberately continued life history, an attitude toward her talents (and handicaps) which implies a revised self-understanding and allows for a *productive* response to the initial situation. This situation, by the way, is not unlike that of a clone who, by being modeled on the person and the life history of a "twin" chronologically out of phase, is deprived of an un-obstructed future of his own.[54]

Eugenic interventions aiming at enhancement reduce ethical freedom insofar as they tie down the person concerned to rejected, but irreversible intentions of third parties, barring him from the spontaneous self-perception of being the undivided author of his own life. Abilities and skills may be easier to identify with than dispositions, let alone properties, but the only thing that counts for the psychical resonance of the person concerned is the intention associated with the programming enterprise. Only in the negative case of the prevention of extreme and highly generalized evils may we have good reasons to assume that the person concerned would consent to the eugenic goal.

Liberal eugenics would not only affect the capacity of "being oneself." It would at the same time create an inter-personal relationship for which there is no precedent. The irreversible choice a person makes for the desired makeup of the genome of another person initiates a type of relationship between these two which jeopardizes a pre-condition for the moral self-understanding of autonomous actors. A universalistic understanding of law and morality rests on the assumption that there is no definite obstacle to egalitarian interpersonal relations. Of course, our societies are marked by manifest as well as structural vio-lence. They are impregnated by the micropower of silent repression, disfigured by despotic suppression, deprivation of political rights, social disempowerment, and economic exploitation. However, we could not be scandalized by this if we did not know that these shameful conditions might *also* be *different*. The conviction that all actors, as persons, obtain the same normative status and are held to deal with one another in mutual and symmetrical recognition rests on the assumption that there is, in principle, a reversibil-ity to interpersonal relationships. No dependence on another person must be irreversible. With genetic pro-gramming, however, a relationship emerges that is asymmetrical in more than one respect – a specific type of paternalism.

Unlike the social dependence inherent in the parent–child relationship, which will, as the generations succeed one another, be resolved with the children growing up, the children's *genealogical* dependence on their parents is, of course, also irreversible. Parents beget their children, children do not beget their parents. But this dependence only engages the children's existence, which as such lends itself only to a curiously abstract form of reproach, not their essence – no qualitative determination of any kind of their future life. In contrast to social dependence, genetic dependence of the person programmed on her designer is concentrated, it is true, in a single attributable act. But in the context of eugenic practice, acts of this type – by omission as well as by execution – lay the grounds for a social relationship in which the usual "reciprocity between persons of equal birth" is revoked.[55] The program designer carries out a one-sided act for which there can be no well-founded assumption of consent, disposing over the genetic factors of another in the paternalistic intention of setting the course, in relevant respects, of the life history of the dependent person. The latter may interpret, but not revise or undo this intention. The consequences are irreversible because the paternalistic intention is laid down in a disarming genetic program instead of being communicatively mediated by a socializing practice which can be subjected to reappraisal by the person "raised."

The irreversible nature of the consequences arising from one-sided acts of genetic manipulation saddles the person who thinks himself capable of making this choice with a problematical responsibility. But must it *per se* act as a restriction on the moral autonomy of the person concerned? All persons, including those born naturally, are in one way or another dependent on their genetic program. There must be a different reason for dependence on a *deliberately* fixed genetic program to be relevant for the programmed person. He is principally barred from exchanging roles with his designer. The product cannot, to put it bluntly, draw up a design for its designer. Our concern with programming here is not whether it will restrict another person's ethical freedom and capacity of being himself, but whether, and how, it might eventually preclude a symmetrical relationship between the programmer and the product thus "designed". Eugenic programming establishes a permanent dependence between persons who know that one of them is principally barred from changing *social* places with the other. But this kind of social dependence, which is irreversible because it was established by ascription, is foreign to the reciprocal and symmetrical relations of mutual recognition proper to a moral and legal community of free and equal persons.

Up to now, only persons born, not persons made, have participated in social interaction. In the biopolitical future prophesied by liberal eugenicists, this horizontal connection would be superseded by an intergenerational stream of action and communication cutting vertically across the deliberately modified genome of future generations.

Now, one might be tempted to think that the democratic constitutional state is, after all, best equipped to provide the framework as well as the means for compensating for this lack of intergenerational reciprocity, by institutionalizing procedures to reestablish the disrupted symmetry on the level of generalized norms. Wouldn't legal norms, if they were established on the broad basis of ethical and political will formation, relieve parents from the dubious responsibility for an individual choice made solely according to their own preferences? Wouldn't legitimacy based on a generalized democratic will remove the stigma of paternalism from parents who mold the genetic fate of their child according to their own preferences, and restore the persons concerned to their status of equal birth? Once these persons are included as democratic co-authors of a legal ruling in a transgenerational consensus by which the asymmetry, irreparable in the individual case, is redressed on a higher level of the common will, they would no longer need to see themselves as persons confined to dependence.

This thought experiment, however, shows why this attempt at reparation must fail. The political consensus required would be either too strong or too weak. Too strong, because a *binding* commitment to collective goals going beyond the prevention of evils agreed upon would be an unconstitutional intervention in the private autonomy of citizens; too weak, because the mere *permission* to make use of eugenic procedures would not be able to relieve parents of their moral responsibility for their highly personal choice of eugenic goals, since the problematic consequence of restricting ethical freedom cannot be ruled out. In the context of a democratically constituted pluralistic society where every citizen has an equal right to an autonomous conduct of life, practices of enhancing eugenics cannot be "normalized" in a legitimate way, because the selection of desirable dispositions cannot be *a priori* dissociated from the prejudgment of specific life-projects.

VII Setting the pace for a self-instrumentalization of the species?

What, then, follows from this analysis for the current debate on stem cell research and PGD? In a first step I have tried, in section II, to explain why the hope of resolving the controversy with one single, compelling argument is an illusion. From a philosophical perspective, extending the argument for human rights to cover human life "from the very beginning" is not at all conclusive. On the other hand, the legal distinction established between the human dignity of the person, which is unconditionally valid, and the protection of the life of the embryo, which may on principle be weighed against other rights, by no means opens the way to a hopeless controversy over conflicting ethical goals. In evaluating prepersonal human life we are not dealing, as I have shown in section III, with a "good" among other goods. How we deal with human life before birth (or with human beings after death) touches on our self-understanding as members of the species. And this self-understanding as members of the species is closely interwoven with our self-understanding as moral persons. Our conceptions of – and attitude toward – prepersonal human life embed the rational morality of subjects of human rights in the stabilizing context of an ethics of the species. This context must endure if morality itself is not to start slipping.

Against the background of a potential liberal eugenics, this internal relation between the ethics of the protection of life and our self-understanding as autonomous beings having equal rights and abiding by moral reasons comes into clearer focus. The moral reasons that hypothetically speak against such a practice cast a shadow also on the practices which open the way to it. Today, we must ask ourselves whether later generations will eventually come to terms with the fact that they may no longer see themselves as the undivided authors of their life – nor will be called upon as such. Will they accept an interpersonal relationship that is no longer consistent with the egalitarian premises of morality and law? And would not, then, the grammatical form of our moral language game – the self-understanding of speakers and actors as beings for whom normative reasons count – be changed as a whole? The arguments I laid out in sections IV to VI were to make plausible the fact that we have to face these questions today, in anticipation of the further advances of genetic engineering. There is, after all, the alarming prospect of a practice of genetic interventions aiming at the modification of traits which will go beyond the boundaries of the essentially communicative relationship between doctor and patient, parents and children, and undermine, through eugenic self-transformation, our normatively structured forms of life.

Such are the concerns which may explain the impression we have when analyzing debates on bioethics, including those in the Bundestag. Participants in this discourse whose contributions rely on standard ways of weighing competing goods (as did those of the representatives of the Liberal Democrats) seem to be out of step. It is not that unconditional existential rigor, as set against the weighing of interests, would be *a priori* superior to the balancing of interests. But many of us seem to have the intuition that we should not *weigh* human life, not even in its earliest stages, either against the freedom (and competitiveness) of research, or against the concern with safeguarding an industrial edge, or against the wish for a healthy child, or even against the prospect (assumed *arguendo*) of new treatments for severe genetic diseases. What is it that is indicated by such an intuition, if we assume that human life does not from the very beginning enjoy the same absolute protection of life that holds for the person?

Concerns as to PGD can be justified more directly than the comparatively archaic inhibition we feel toward research involving the destruction of embryos. Our unwillingness to legalize PGD is grounded in consideration of both the conditional creation of embryos and the nature of this condition itself. Bringing about a situation in which we might eventually reject an afflicted embryo is as dubious as selection according to criteria defined by one side only. Selection in this case cannot but be one-sided, and therefore instrumentalizing, because there can be no assumption of an anticipated consent which, as in cases of genetic manipulation for therapeutic ends, may at least be confirmed by later statements of the treated patients: here, no person is created in the first place. In contrast to

68

embryonic research, moral weighing in this case may, after all, be brought to bear against the degree of severe suffering the future person herself can be expected to face.[56] The advocates of a ruling which might eventually limit the admissibility of the procedure to a few unambiguously extreme cases of monogenetic diseases may primarily[57] argue against the protection of life by pointing out that preventing an unbearably restricted future life is in the best interest, advocationally attended to, of the future person concerned.

But even so, the fact that we make a highly momentous distinction between life worth living and life not worth living *for others* remains disconcerting. Do parents who decide to rely on embryo selection, in view of their own wish for a child, fail to adopt a clinical attitude, which is oriented toward the goal of healing? Or is their attitude toward the unborn child that of dealing with a second person, albeit uncontrollably fictitious – on the assumption that this person himself would refuse an existence subject to specific restrictions? I am not sure myself; but even so, the opponents would still have strong reasons for pointing out (as the Federal President did recently) the discriminating side-effects and the problematic normalization likely to occur as a corollary to any evaluation, restrictive as it may be, of a form of life presumed to be handicapped.

The situation will be different when the advances of genetic engineering some day allow genetic intervention to be carried out in a therapeutic perspective subsequent to a diagnosis of severe hereditary handicaps and, thus, make selection unnecessary. This would, of course, mean that we have crossed the threshold to negative eugenics. But in this case, the reasons which today, as pointed out above, are invoked in favor of lifting the ban on PGD could be brought to bear on gene-modifying interventions without compelling us to weigh an undesirable handicap against the protection of the life of a "rejected" embryo. A genetic manipulation (carried out, preferably, on somatic cells) restricted to clearly therapeutic goals can be compared to the combat against epidemics and other widespread diseases. The depth of intervention inherent to the operative means does not justify abstention from treatment.

A more complex explanation is required for the disgust we feel at the notion that research involving the destruction of embryos is instrumentalizing human life in view of the benefits (and profits) to be derived from a scientific progress which is not even predictable with any certainty. What is expressed here is the attitude that "an embryo – even if created in vitro – [is] the future child of future parents, and nothing else. It is not available for other ends" (Margot von Renesse). This attitude, insofar as it exists independently from ontological beliefs about the beginning of personal life, does not seek justification in terms of a metaphysically conceived human dignity. It is, however, no less impervious to the moral argument which I have raised against liberal eugenics, in any case if used directly. The intuition that the embryo must not be instrumentalized for arbitrary *other* ends, it is true, leads to the claim that it be treated in anticipation as a second person who, *were* she to be born, *could* assume an attitude toward this treatment. But the purely experimental or "destructive" use in the research laboratory does not aim at birth at all. In which sense, then, can it "fail to meet" the clinical attitude proper to the dealings with a being whose later consent may at least in principle be presupposed?

Reference to the collective good of treatments likely to be developed obscures the fact that this implies an instrumentalization incompatible with the clinical attitude. Of course, research involving the destruction of embryos cannot be justified from the clinical point of view of healing, because the latter is tailored to therapeutic dealings with second persons. The clinical perspective, rightly understood, individualizes. But why should the standard

70

of a virtual doctor–patient relationship apply to research conducted in the laboratory at all? If this counterquestion does not take us back to the essentialist controversy over the "real" destiny of embryonic life, there indeed seems to be no alternative to an open-ended weighing of goods. The only way for this controversial issue not to end up in an ordinary process of weighing is to accord prepersonal life, as I have tried to explain in section III, a *specific* weight of its own.

This, now, is where the long-prepared argument comes in that the advances of genetic engineering tend to blur the deeply rooted categorical distinctions between the subjective and the objective, the grown and the made. What is at stake, therefore, with the instrumentalization of prepersonal life is the ethical self-understanding of the species, which is crucial for whether or not we may go on to see ourselves as beings committed to moral judgment and action. Where we lack compelling *moral* reasons, we have to let ourselves be guided by the signposts set up by the *ethics* of the species.[58]

Let us suppose that, with research involving the destruction of embryos, a practice will come to prevail for which the protection of prepersonal human life is secondary to "other ends", even if these ends consisted in nothing more than the prospect of developing high-ranking collective goods (such as new medical treatments). The desensitization of the way we look at human nature, going hand in hand with the *normalization* of this practice, would clear the path for liberal eugenics. Here we can already discern the future *fait accompli*, by then a fact of the past, which later apologists will be able to refer to as the Rubicon that was crossed. Looking at a possible future for human nature makes us aware of the present need for regulation. Normative barriers in our dealings with embryos are the result of the point of view taken by a moral community of persons that fends off the pace-makers of a self-instrumentalization of the species in order to safeguard – let us say: out of concern for itself, but in

71

the broader perspective of the ethics of the species – its communicatively structured form of life.

Embryonic research and PGD stir up our emotions mainly because they *exemplify* a danger which is associated with the perspective of "human breeding." By depriving the fusion of two sets of chromosomes of its contingency, the intergenerational relations lose the naturalness which so far has been a part of the taken-for-granted background of our self-understanding as a species. If we abstain from "moralizing" human nature, we might see the emergence of a dense intergenerational stream of cumulative decisions cutting across the contemporary networks of interaction in a one-directional, vertical way. Whereas the effective history of cultural traditions and formation processes unfolds, as Gadamer has shown, in the medium of questions and answers, genetic programs would give future generations no opportunity to respond in the same way. Getting used to having human life biotechnologically at the disposal of our contingent preferences cannot help but change our normative self-understanding.

In this perspective, the two controversial innovations, even while still at their initial stage, make us aware of how our lives might be changed if genetic interventions aiming at the modification of traits were to *become normal practice*, emancipating themselves entirely from the context of the therapy of individual persons. It could, then, no longer be ruled out that alien and, in this case, genetically fixed intentions take possession, through enhancing eugenic interventions, of the life history of the programmed person. This is why the question of whether and how an act thus reified affects our capacity of being ourselves, as well as our relation to others, is so disconcerting. Will we still be able to come to a self-understanding as persons who are the undivided authors of their own lives, and approach others, without exception, as persons of equal birth? With this, two presuppositions of our moral self-understanding, spelled out in terms of an ethics of the species, are at stake.

This fact, however, can account for the heat of the current controversy only as long as belonging to a moral community is still a vital interest. It cannot be taken for granted, after all, that we will still *want* this status of a member of a community that requires all its members to show equal respect for every other member and to be responsible in their solidarity with all of them. That we *shall* act morally is inscribed in the very sense of a (deontologically conceived) morality. But why – if biotechnology is subtly undermining our identity as members of the species – should we *want* to be moral? An assessment of morality as a whole is itself not a moral judgment, but an ethical one, a judgment which is part of the ethics of the species.

Without the emotions roused by moral sentiments like obligation and guilt, reproach and forgiveness, without the liberating effect of moral respect, without the happiness felt through solidarity and without the depressing effect of moral failure, without the "friendliness" of a civilized way of dealing with conflict and opposition, we would feel, or so we still think today, that the universe inhabited by men would be unbearable. Life in a moral void, in a form of life empty even of cynicism, would not be worth living. This judgment simply expresses the "impulse" to prefer an existence of human dignity to the coldness of a form of life not informed by moral considerations. The same impulse accounts for the historical transition, which is repeated in ontogenesis, to a posttraditional stage of moral awareness.

When the religious and metaphysical worldviews lost their binding nature and the transition to a tolerated pluralism of worldviews took place, we (or most of us) did not turn out be cool cynics or indifferent relativists, because almost by reflex we held – and *wanted* to hold – to the binary code of moral judgments being right or wrong. We readjusted the practices of the lifeworld and of the political community to the premises of a rational morality and of human rights because they provided the common ground for a humane existence irrespective of any differences arising from the variety of worldviews.[59] Perhaps the affective opposition raised today against a dreaded change in the identity of the species can be explained – and justified – by similar motives.

Postscript (January 2002)

I had the privilege of presenting "The Future of Human Nature" at a colloquium on Law, Philosophy, and Social Theory led by Ronald Dworkin and Thomas Nagel.[60] The objections that these theses encountered, both at this colloquium and later in Germany as well,[61] have given me the occasion for some second thoughts. Even if what I recognize is more a need for explication than revision, I have come to a far clearer awareness of the unplumbed philosophical depths of the debate on the natural foundations for the self-understanding of responsibly acting persons. Even after completing this text, I sense that unclarities remain. My impression is that we still have not reflected deeply enough. Above all, the connection between the contingency of a life's beginning that is not at our disposal and the freedom to give one's life an ethical shape demands a more penetrating analysis.

(1) I would like to begin by noting an interesting difference in the climate and background assumptions of the discussions that I have participated in on both sides of the Atlantic. In Germany, the philosophical discussion is skeptical, often introducing highly normative conceptions of the person and metaphysically loaded conceptions of nature, in arguing the question of *whether* further developments in genetic technology – predominantly in the fields of organ breeding and reproductive medicine – are permissible. In America, by contrast, the discussion focuses primarily on the question of *how* developments that are already taken essentially for granted should be implemented, even insofar as these developments point beyond the application of genetic therapies toward "shopping in the genetic supermarket." It is clear that these technologies will transform the relation between generations. But for the pragmatically minded Americans, these new prac-

tices, while intensifying familiar problems of distributive justice, don't generate any fundamentally new problems of their own.

This more carefree manner of perceiving problems is a result of a still-unbroken trust in scientific and technological development, particularly through the lens of the Lockean liberal tradition. This tradition foregrounds the protection of the individual legal person's freedom of choice against the state, and views threats to this freedom primarily in the vertical dimension of the relation of private members of society to state power. In the face of the overwhelming danger of violating rights in the application of political power, the fear of misused social power – which private persons can exercise in the horizontal dimension of their relations with other private persons – recedes into the background. The unintended side-effects (or *Drittwirkung*) of basic rights are foreign to the understanding of rights in the classical liberal tradition.

From this liberal viewpoint, it virtually goes without saying that decisions regarding the genetic composition of children should not be submitted to any regulation by the state, but rather should be left to the parents. This would suggest that the new freedom of choice opened up by genetic technologies should ultimately be understood as an extension of reproductive freedom and parental rights; that is, of individual rights which persons validly maintain against the state. An entirely different viewpoint emerges if we conceive of rights held by individual subjects as the mirror image of an objective legal order which obliges state authorities to observe their duties to protect weaker or helpless parts of society. This applies to the cases of protecting the life of the unborn, who are unable to protect their individual rights by themselves. This shift in perspective brings to the foreground objective principles that are embodied in the legal order as a whole. Objective right realizes and interprets the basic idea of the mutual recognition of free and equal persons who voluntarily associate with one another in order to legitimately regulate their common life through the means of positive law.

From the point of view of the constitution of a political community, the vertical relations between citizens and the state are no longer privileged over the horizontal network of relations that citizens maintain with one another. In light of our problem, the question is how parents' rights to make eugenic decisions will affect their genetically programmed children, and whether the consequences of these decisions infringe upon the objectively protected well-being of the future child.

Of course, parents' rights to determine genetic features of their children would only conflict with the basic rights of another person if the in vitro embryo were already "another," who possessed completely valid basic rights. This question – currently under debate by German legal scholars – can hardly be answered in the affirmative given the premises of an ethically neutral constitutional order.[62] I have proposed that we distinguish the *inviolability* of human dignity [*Menschenwürde*], as established in Article 1, Section 1 of the German Basic Law, from the *nondisposability* of prepersonal human life. This nondisposability, in turn, can be taken in the sense of a *gradated protection of human life [abgestufter Lebensschutz]*, under the terms of the Basic Law Article 2, Section 2, which keeps the basic right to protection of human life and bodily integrity open for a specification by statute. But if no right to unconditional protection of life or unconditional protection from bodily harm can be assumed at the moment of genetic intervention, then the argument against the *Drittwirkung* – the potentially harmful consequences – of the exercise of parental rights has no *direct* application.

The unintended consequences that a eugenic intervention can have are, in any event, of an indirect nature. They would not harm the rights of an existing person, but rather risk to reduce the status of a future one. In the preceding text I have developed the view that the person

77

whose genetic composition has been prenatally altered may, upon learning of the design for her genetic makeup, experience difficulties in understanding herself as an autonomous and equal member of an association of free and equal persons. According to this view, there cannot exist any *direct* collision between the rights of parents, extended to the opportunities for eugenic interventions, and the legally guaranteed well-being of the child. However, the parents' decisions might *indirectly* have an adverse effect on the sense of her autonomy, that is on the moral self-understanding which must be expected from every member of a legal community, if persons are to have the same chances to make use of equally distributed individual rights. In this sense, the potential harm lies not at the level of a deprivation of the rights of a legal person, but rather in the uncertain status of a person as a bearer of potential rights. With the realization of the noncontingency of her manufactured biological origins, the young person risks losing a mental presupposition for assuming a status necessary for her, as a legal person, to actually enjoy equal civil rights.

These cursory remarks are not intended as an entry into a legal debate. In any event, while those different perspectives arise from differences between the constitutional traditions of various nations, they have common roots in the contractarian tradition and rest on the common foundation of an egalitarian universalism. The transatlantic comparison between two differing legal cultures was only meant to serve as a heuristic tool for a juridical illustration of those two conceptual levels that now interest me in view of a *moral evaluation* of the consequences of "liberal eugenics." This term refers to a practice that entrusts interventions into the genome of an embryo to the discretion of the parents. Such a practice does not imply any immediate intervention into the freedom to which each naturally born person is entitled, regardless of whether she has been naturally fathered or genetically programmed. But it does touch upon a natural *presupposition* for the self-understanding of the affected person as an autonomous and responsible agent. In the preceding text I primarily concentrated on two *possible* consequences: first, that genetically programmed persons might no longer regard themselves as the sole authors of their own life history; and second, that they might no longer regard themselves as unconditionally equal-born persons in relation to previous generations.

If we want to pinpoint these potential harms correctly, we need to project onto the moral universe that two-level juridical model of a community in which one must first assume the status of a member in an association of free and equal legal persons before one can possess and exercise any *particular* right. According to this model, eugenic practices, while they are not *directly* intervening into the genetically modified person's spheres of free action, might well harm the status of the future person as a member of the universe of moral beings. Within this "kingdom of ends," certainly, nobody – except in his simultaneous role as an autonomous participant in joint self-legislation – is subjected to general laws. In the moral universe, subjection of a person to the unjustly imposed arbitrary will of another one is ruled out. But such an imposition from within a community, even if it is excluded from the relationships obtaining between morally acting persons, must nevertheless not be confused with an external or alien determination of the natural and mental constitution of a *future* person, prior to an entry into the moral community. Intervention into the prenatal distribution of genetic resources means a redefinition of those naturally fixed ranges of opportunities and scopes for possible decision within which the future person will one day use her freedom to give her own life its ethical shape.

In what follows I want to take up four objections (or better, four sets of objections) to this claim. The first directly challenges the cause–effect relation between the practices of an improving eugenics and the "alien determination," even if always indirect, of a future person. (2) The second objection takes issue with my weighted choice of the exemplary case – a partial alteration of genetic features that leaves the identity of the affected being intact. (3) The third objection casts doubt on the premises of postmetaphysical thinking, and recommends instead the adoption of rather strongly ontological background assumptions for the "species-ethical" context in which morality should be embedded. (4) Finally, I take up the question of whether arguments against eugenic practices which, at this point, are still not even up for discussion, allow us to draw any meaningful implications for current controversies surrounding preimplantation genetic diagnosis and applied (consummatory?) embryo research.

(2) Thomas Nagel, Thomas McCarthy and others think it is essentially counterintuitive to expect that the changed features or characteristics that result from a genetic intervention would ever be experienced as an interference of somebody else into one's own life, thereby also undermining the principle of equality between generations. Why should it make any difference for the moral person, within the network of her interpersonal relationships, whether her genetic inheritance depended on the vagaries of her parents' choice of partners and the work of nature, or from the decisions of a designer whose preferences are beyond her influence? In other words, anyone who participates in the language game of morality has to rely on specific pragmatic presuppositions.[63] Morally judging and acting subjects attribute mutual accountability to one another; they ascribe both to themselves and all others the capacity to lead an autonomous life, and expect solidarity and equal respect from each other. If the moral order is thus symbolically generated and reproduced by participants themselves, it is hard to see how someone's moral

status can be harmed by the artificiality of her genetic composition.

It is, of course, implausible to assume that the objectifying attitude of the programmer-parents toward the embryo in vitro would continue on into an objectifying relation with the programmed person after birth. D. Birnbacher refers to the example of test-tube babies who have grown to adulthood; he rightly argues that in a society that made eugenic practices or reproductive cloning procedures generally available, we would not necessarily have any difficulties in recognizing genetically altered children or clones as "free and equal interaction partners." But this is not really the point of the argument against alien determination. It doesn't refer to a form of discrimination that the affected person experiences in her social surroundings, but rather to a prenatally induced self-devaluation; to a harm to her own moral self-understanding. What is affected is a subjective qualification essential for assuming the status of a full member of a moral community.

The designer, choosing according to his own preferences (or social habits), does not violate the moral rights of another person. His intervention does not mean that he would be disadvantaging another person in the distribution of basic goods, or depriving him of legitimate opportunities, or forcing him to perform particular practices from which others are excused. Instead, he changes the initial conditions for the identity formation of another person in an asymmetrical and irrevocable manner. There is no constraint of another's freedom to give shape to her own life on an interpersonal level – a level where one person could oppress another one. But as the designer makes himself the *co-author of the life of another*, he intrudes – from the interior, one could say – into the other's consciousness of her own autonomy. The programmed person, being no longer certain about the contingency of the natural roots of her life history,[64] may feel the lack of a mental precondition for coping with the moral expectation to take, even if only in retrospect, the *sole* responsibility for her own life.

Insofar as the genetically altered person feels that the scope for a possible use of her ethical freedom has been intentionally changed by a prenatal design, she may suffer from the consciousness of sharing the authorship of her own life and her own destiny with someone else. This sort of *alienating* dilution or fracturing of one's own identity is a sign that an important boundary has become permeable – the deontological shell which assures the inviolability of the person, the uniqueness of the individual, and the irreplaceability of one's own subjectivity. The space in the relationship between generations, which makes the young adult independent of her parents, can disappear in this way as well. But without this independence, a form of reciprocal recognition based on strict equality is no longer possible. Three more specific counterarguments have been mustered against this scenario of a no longer open future in which one's own life plans collide with the genetically fixed intentions of another.

(2a) Why shouldn't a young person struggle with manipulated genetic predispositions in the same way as with naturally acquired ones? Why, for example, couldn't she let a talent for mathematics lie unused in the one case just as in the other, if she preferred to become a musician or a professional athlete? The difference between the two cases, of course, is that the preference of the parents to furnish their child with *this* genetic inheritance and not another has now become part of the domain of decisions for which one must assume responsibility. Exercising the power to dispose over the genetic predispositions of a future person means that from that point on, each person, whether she has been genetically programmed or not, can regard her own genome as the consequence of a criticizable action *or omission*. The young person can call his designer to account, and demand a justification for why,

in deciding on this or that genetic inheritance, the designer *failed* to choose athletic ability or musical talent, which would have been vastly more useful for the career that she had actually chosen to pursue. This scenario raises the question of whether we can ever assume the responsibility for the distribution of natural talents, and for that range of opportunities within which another person is able to freely develop and pursue her own conception of life.

(2b) This argument certainly loses much of its force if it can be shown that the distinction between natural and social fate is less razor sharp than the way we usually understand it. The goal-directed choice of partners, guided by phenotypical characteristics (according to the model of horse breeding) is not an illuminating case in point. More relevant is the case of an athletically or musically gifted child who can develop into a champion tennis player or a successful soloist if her proud parents recognize and foster her talent at the right time. The parents must help develop their child's talent through discipline and practice at an early point of cognitive development when only parental drilling is a possibility and not yet an "offer" the child could accept or reject. Let's imagine that in this case the young adult actually has entirely different life plans, and rebukes her parents for the torments of (what seems to her) wholly useless training imposed on her, or another who feels neglected by his parents' failure to encourage him early enough, and then rubs his parents' noses in this failure for leaving his natural talents untapped.

Let us assume, in the sense of a thought experiment, that it is hardly possible to distinguish the consequences of such pedagogical interventions from corresponding eugenic interventions (which may in fact only serve to reduce the difficulties of training). What forms the *tertium comparationis* is the irrevocability of choices that proved decisive in setting the course of the life history of another person. Unlike those stages of maturation which explain

83

why children respond to requisite pedagogical stimuli with accelerated learning processes only at a specific age, in our case we are supposing not a support (or omitted support) for *general* cognitive development, but rather a *special* influence that has consequences precisely for the future course of an individual's life history. But then the question remains whether such cases of too much or too little training are appropriate counterexamples. These cases – each in its own context, and from the perspective of the person affected by them – can represent either repression or neglect, either overdrilling the child or failing to support him. But do they point to fundamentally different problems than those we could expect to arise from genetic modifications?

Though they affect social rather than organic processes, these training programs stand at least in the same line with comparable genetic programming, both in terms of the irreversibility and the specificity of their consequences for the life history of individuals. Insofar as they can be criticized on the same grounds, the one sort of practice can't be invoked as a way of disburdening the other one from the same objections. To the degree that parents are rebuked for imposing specific pedagogical practices on their children (because they are prejudicing capabilities that can have *ambivalent* consequences within the unpredictable context of their child's future life), the designer of genetic programs is all the more reproachable for usurping the responsibility for the life of a future person, a responsibility that has to be reserved for this person herself, if her consciousness of autonomy is to remain intact. The dubiousness of forms of early training – supposing they are in fact irreversible, despite their unforeseeable consequences for the life history of the affected – illuminates from the other side the very same normative background which casts doubts on corresponding eugenic practices. For in this background we find the irreducible ethical responsibility that one bears for one's own life, and the assumption (even if counterfactual) that each of us is able to appropriate our own life histories critically, rather than being doomed to the fatalistic acceptance of the consequences of socialization.

(2c) The argument against an alien co-authorship for one's own life only works, of course, if we assume that the child's genetic constitution, chosen from among other alternatives, actually *reduces* the range of her future life choices. But the danger of prescribing a particular range of identities clearly decreases (if we give free rein to our imagination) in the sequence of properties (such as hair color, body size or "beauty" in general), dispositions (docility versus aggressiveness, or "ego strength"), capacities (athletic grace and stamina, or musical talent) and "basic genetic goods" (i.e. highly generalized capacities such as bodily strength, intelligence, or memory). Dieter Birnbacher and others find no plausible reasons for the assumption that a person would refuse, in hindsight, an *expansion* of their resources and a *higher level* of genetic basic goods.[65]

Here too, however, we face the question of whether we can ever know if a given, particular genetic endowment in fact *expands* the latitude that another person has for giving shape to her own life. Can parents wanting only the best for their child ever really presume to know all the circumstances – and the various interactions of these circumstances with each other – in which a brilliant memory, for example, or high intelligence (however defined) will prove a benefit for their child? A good memory is often but by no means always a blessing. Not being able to forget can be a curse. The sense of relevance and the formative power of traditions depend on the selectivity of our memories. Sometimes an overloaded storage hinders us from dealing productively with new data to be taken in.

The same is true for outstanding intelligence. In many situations it is a predictable advantage. But how will the "head start" of high intelligence play itself out in a competitive society – for example, in the character formation of the highly talented person? How will such a person interpret her differential talent and put it to use: with calm and control, or ceaseless ambition? How will she come to terms with a capability that both marks her and may provoke the envy of others? Not even the highly general good of bodily health maintains one and the same value within the contexts of different life histories. Parents can't even know whether a mild physical handicap may not prove in the end to be an advantage for their child.

(3) This is the viewpoint from which I can respond to the objections against what I have described as an exemplary case of the alteration of genetic characteristics. Ronald Dworkin has challenged me with a very instructive variation of the four conditions that my thought experiment had tacitly assumed: (a) the genetic intervention is carried out by a second person, and not by the affected person herself; (b) the affected person maintains retrospective awareness of the prenatal intervention, and (c) understands herself as someone altered in some genetic features or characteristics, but remaining identical with herself, so that she can assume a hypothetical attitude toward the genetic intervention itself, while (d) she refuses to appropriate the modified genetic makeup as a "part of herself."

(ad a) The argument against alien determination becomes irrelevant if we imagine the affected person being able to painlessly revoke a genetic intervention carried out conditionally, so to speak, before her birth, or that she chose on her own to have the genetic intervention performed, in the manner of somatic cell therapy – which would then not really be different from cases of cosmetic surgery. This variant of self-manipulation is helpful because it clarifies the postmetaphysical meaning of the argument. My criticism is not rooted in some fundamental mistrust of the analysis and artificial recombination of the components of the human genome as such. In other words, the argument doesn't proceed on the assumption that the technicization of "inner nature" constitutes something like a transgression of natural boundaries. The criticism remains valid quite independently of the idea of a "natural" or even "holy" order, which can be sacrilegiously "overstepped."

Instead, the argument against alien determination draws its strength completely from the fact that a genetic designer, acting according to his own preferences, assumes an irrevocable role in determining the contours of the life history and identity of another person, while remaining unable to assume even her counterfactual consent. This is an invasion in the deontologically protected core of a future person, whom nobody can acquit of the expectation of one day taking her existence into her own hands, and leading her life exclusively under her own direction.

(ad b) Of course, a conflict between one's own life plans and the genetically fixed intentions of another can only arise if the young person is aware of the design of the prenatal intervention. Must one therefore conclude that no harm results if this information is withheld? This suspicion lures us down a false path of an ontological attempt to localize the injury to autonomy, independently of any conflict awareness, in the "unconscious" of the affected person, or at a "vegetative" stratum of the organism that remains inaccessible to consciousness. This variant – a *concealed* genetic intervention – merely raises the moral question of whether it is permissible to withhold from someone the knowledge of a biographically significant fact (such as the identity of parents, for example). But it is hardly permitted to forestall the identity crises of a young person in such a way that one takes the precaution of concealing from him precisely the causal history of the anticipated problem, thereby adding to the programming itself the deception over this relevant fact of life.

(ad c)   Of course, we can alter the thought experiment so that the genetic programming extends over the identity of the future person *in its entirety*. For example, selecting the gender of one's child is an option already available today through preimplantation genetic diagnosis.[66] Now, one can hardly imagine that the boy (or girl) who learns of the prenatal selection of his own gender could plausibly confront his parents with the honest objection "I would rather have been a girl (or a boy)." It's not as if such fantasies didn't exist. But (if we assume a "normal" acquisition of gender role) these fantasies carry no *moral* weight. Apart from the very special indications for a transgendering procedure for adults, adolescent wishes for a change in sexual identity appear as an "empty abstraction," since the person involved can never project his own identity back to a gender-neutral past. A person *is* a man or woman; *has* this or that gender – and could not assume the other gender without at the same time becoming *another* person. If identity cannot be maintained, then there is no fixed point of reference of *one and the same* person who could maintain her own continuity while looking back before the parental intervention, and who could *herself* oppose it.

The individual life history of a person may provide good ethical reasons for *leading* a different kind of life, but not for wanting to *be* another person – the project of transforming oneself into an entirely other person remains tied to the powers of imagination of the actual person herself. A decision as profoundly significant for identity as the choice of gender thus appears to encounter no serious objection from the person affected by it. But if this is true for the determination of an *identity-generating* characteristic – so the objection runs – then we are in no position to object to the genetic modification of *any* properties, dispositions, or capabilities. However, this response [*arguendo*] of Dworkin's is plausible only at first glance.

A genetic intervention can be open to criticism from someone not directly affected by it, even when the affected person herself is not in a position to exercise the criticism. In our example, the identity-generating choice of gender draws its apparent innocuousness from an intuitive prohibition against discrimination: Because there is no moral reason for the preference of one gender over another, it *should* make no difference for the affected person whether he or she has come into the world as a boy or a girl. But it does not follow from this that a genetic program which (rather like the creation of a Golem) stretches over the *entire* biological identity of a future person – which would constitute the person "from the ground up" – would for that reason be immune from all criticism. To be sure, this criticism could no longer be leveled by the affected person herself, as it still could in the case of a transformation of a particular genetic feature. Such a partial genetic modification leaves an identity intact that the person herself can retrospectively trace back and maintain beyond the event of that intervention.

For these reasons, it seems reasonable to adopt the point of view of a young person who finds herself in a situation defined by the four conditions listed above. In such a case, namely, the alien determination manifests itself in the potential for dissent between the affected person and the designer over the intentions of the genetic intervention itself. The moral reason for this objection remains unchanged, of course, if the person whose consciousness of autonomy has been harmed does not herself articulate the objection simply because she cannot do so. Surely we have a duty to protect others from harm to the best of our ability. We should come to the aid of others, and do all we can to improve the conditions of their lives. But we are not permitted to determine, according to our own ideas about other people's future life, the range of opportunities these others will one day face in their attempt to give ethical shape to their own lives. Even in the best of cases, our finite spirit doesn't possess the kind of prognostic knowledge that enables us to judge the consequences of genetic interventions within the context of a future life history of another human being.

Can we know what is potentially good for another? This may be so in particular cases. But even then our knowledge remains fallible, and may be applied only in the form of clinical suggestions for somebody whom the advisor already knows as an individuated being. Irrevocable decisions over the genetic design of an unborn person are always presumptuous. A person who potentially stands to benefit from such a decision must always preserve the ability to say no. Since we can have no objective knowledge of values beyond moral insight, and since a first person perspective is inscribed in all of our ethical knowledge, we overtax the finite constitution of the human spirit by expecting that we can determine which sort of genetic inheritance will be "the best" for the lives of our children.

(ad d)   As citizens in a democratic community, which must legally regulate practices of eugenic intervention, we surely will not be able to disburden ourselves from the task of anticipating the possible agreement or refusal of those affected by eugenic practices – not, in any event, if we want to permit therapeutic genetic interventions (or even selections) in cases of serious genetic disorders in the interests of the handicapped themselves. The pragmatic objections to the entire project of separating positive from negative eugenics which insist on the fluid boundary between both are based upon plausible examples. And it is as plausible to predict an effect of cumulative familiarization that will push the limits of tolerance for genetic interventions already regarded as "normal" ever further toward more and more demanding norms of health. However, there is a regulative idea that establishes a standard for determining a boundary, one which is surely in need of continuous interpretation, but which is not

basically contestable: All therapeutic genetic interventions, including prenatal ones, must remain dependent
on consent that is at least counterfactually attributed to
those possibly affected by them.

Public discussions among citizens on the permissibility
of such negative eugenic measures will be touched off
anew each time lawmakers propose another entry on the
list of indicated genetic disorders. Each new authorization
of a prenatal therapeutic genetic intervention constitutes
a tremendous burden for those parents who have principled reasons for not wanting to make use of the license.
Whoever deviates from a permitted or even a familiarized
eugenic practice, and takes the risk of an avoidable birth
defect into the bargain, has to fear accusations of neglect,
and possibly the resentment of their own child.

In anticipating these consequences, requirements for
justification (which confront the lawmaker at each step
in this path) are fortunately quite high. Though the terms
of the debates remain different, the general opinion- and
will-formation will be just as deeply polarized as it was in
the abortion debate.

(4) The dangers of constraining the ethical freedom of a
genetically modified person can never be ruled out a priori
as long as the intervention is performed one-sidedly, that
is, no longer with the clinical attitude toward another
person whose consent has always to be secured. Attribut-
ing such consent can only be justified in cases where there
is a certain prognosis of extreme suffering. We can only
expect a consensus among otherwise highly divergent
value orientations in the face of the challenge to prevent
extreme evils rejected by everybody. I have, in the preceding text, described the problematic case of a young
person who retrospectively learns of a genetic programming carried out before her own birth, and who cannot
identify with the genetically fixed intentions of her
parents. The danger for such a person is that she is no
longer capable of understanding herself as the undivided

91

author of her own life, and thus feels bound by the chains of the previous generation's genetic decisions.

Certainly decisions of this kind, reaching straight through a person's socialization as a whole, affect the ethical freedom in an *indirect* manner. They risk disqualifying the harmed person *for* an unconditioned participation in the language game of moral life, without immediately interfering with the relations among participants themselves. We can only take part in the moral language game under the idealizing presupposition that each of us carries the sole responsibility for giving ethical shape to his or her own life, and enjoys equal treatment with complete reciprocity of rights and duties. But if eugenic manipulation changes the rules of the language game itself, this act can no longer be criticized according to those rules.[67] Therefore, liberal eugenics provokes the question of how to value morality as a whole.

The morality of egalitarian universalism stands in question as such. To be sure, this modern form of moral consciousness provides the only rationally acceptable basis for the normative regulation of action conflicts in pluralist societies. But why shouldn't complex societies simply drop their normative foundations entirely, and switch over to systemic(!) (or, in the future, biogenetic) steering mechanisms? No arguments from the moral language game itself can be mustered against a eugenic self-instrumentalization of the human species which changes the very rules of the game. All that remains at the appropriate level of argumentation are morally self-reflective, that is, species-ethical considerations on the organic (and, in their consequences, the mental) presuppositions necessary for the moral self-understanding of responsibly acting persons. However, species-ethical considerations of this kind dispense with the presumptively compelling force of strong moral reasons.

Regarding the question of the identity of man as a species-being, we see a competition between several conceptions. Naturalistic versions of humanity, spelled out in the languages of physics, neurology, or evolutionary biology, have long clashed with the classical image of humanity derived from religion and metaphysics. Today, the relevant controversy is played out between a naturalistic futurism, committed to a technical self-optimization of human beings, and anthropological conceptions whose "weak naturalism" has them accept the views of neo-Darwinism (and scientific views in general) without scientistically undermining or constructivistically outstripping the normative self-understanding of speakers and actors, for whom reasons still count.[68] Notwithstanding its higher level of generalization, species-ethical considerations share, along with the ethical-existential reasoning of individuals, and the ethical-political debates within national arenas, the reference to an always particular, and reflexively appropriated life context. Here too, the inquiry of who we are as exemplars of the human species, in view of the relevant anthropological facts, is connected with the evaluative question of how we should understand ourselves.

The we-perspectives of species-*ethical* considerations are not reducible to that single *moral* we-perspective, which, driven by the requirement to generalize interests, emerges as a construct as all those involved reciprocally adopt their mutual perspectives. Unless we fall back on treacherous metaphysical certainties, it is reasonable to expect persisting disagreements in the discourse universe of competing approaches toward a species ethics. Nevertheless, it seems to me that there is one argument that acquires particular weight in the debate over the best ethical self-understanding of our species: not all of the ethical conceptions harmonize with our self-understanding as morally responsible persons to the same degree. It remains a horrifying prospect that a eugenic self-optimization of the species, carried out via the aggregated preferences of consumers in the genetic supermarket (and via society's capacity for forming new habits), might change the moral status of future persons: "Life in a moral vacuum that not even the moral cynic would still recognize, wouldn't be worth living."

This is not itself a moral argument. But it is an argument that appeals to the preconditions for preserving a moral self-understanding of persons as a reason for favoring a species-ethical understanding that cannot be squared with the heedless optimization and self-instrumentalization of prepersonal life.[69] Ludwig Siep formulates this argument in such a way that the preference for the moral form of life (I would prefer to put it as the moral structuring of forms of life) suggests itself as a "species-ethical option."[70] But this argument in no way makes the *validity* of morality dependent on its *cognitive* embeddedness in an appropriate environment of species-ethical beliefs – as if what people regard as morally good had to fit into an ontological framework of "good states of the world."

As long as the moral point of view for what is a just solution to action conflicts prevails, the morality of equal respect for each, and solidarity with all, can be justified from out of the reservoir of rational reasons alone. If morality were still to be grounded in this or that world-view, or if, as Robert Spaemann holds, these two sides, morality and metaphysics, stood in a circular justificatory relation to one another, then we would have to write off the increases in tolerance that were won by an autonomous morality and the conception of human rights. In that case, from the very beginning we would simply have to accept as part of the bargain the absence of any normatively convincing pacification of cultural conflicts and clashes of worldviews.[71]

Egalitarian universalism is widely acknowledged as a great achievement of modernity; in any event, it has not been placed in question by other moralities, or other conceptions of species ethics. It could be toppled only by the silent consequences of practices we will become numbly accustomed to. It is the ceaseless drive of biotechnological development, and not naturalistic worldviews, that undermines the natural (and consequently mental) presuppositions of a form of morality whose status hardly anybody wants to challenge explicitly. This mode of undermining is as much loaded with practical consequences as it is free of theory. What helps in opposing it is the work of *stabilizing* our morality by embedding it in the context of a species-ethical self-understanding which reminds us of the value of egalitarian universalism, and the preconditions for it, before we get accustomed to the insidious revision of as yet self-evident assumptions about the sense of autonomy and of intergenerational equality.

(5) Finally, Ludwig Siep doubts that the warranted reservations about positive eugenics allow us to draw any meaningful conclusions concerning the current decisions on PGD and applied embryo research. Given the constitutional premises that there is no unconditional protection of human life, such counterarguments can at best have the character of "slippery-slope" arguments. And the weight of this kind of argument will vary depending on how great we judge the harm to be that emerges in the hypothetical case of a "breach in the dike" (if we take the German equivalent for "slippery slope") argument, and how probable it is that the criticized step actually leads to the breaking point.

Regarding the first issue, in my experience many of my colleagues regard the prospect of a positive eugenics as an opportunity, rather than a potential harm. Either they remain unconvinced by arguments against alien determination (like Nagel or McCarthy). Or if they are (like Dworkin) moral realists they see the argument as pointless, since they regard selecting genetic features for the sake of the child's welfare a matter of correct moral knowledge. These reactions only support my belief that current controversies over the possible consequences of eugenic practices – which, while still beyond our capacities at present, are nevertheless not entirely unlikely in the future – are anything but idle speculation.

But those who reject such eugenic practices, whether on principled or for the time being on tactical considerations, can still reject slippery-slope arguments in the other respect. PGD and human embryonic stem cell research can only be described as pacemakers toward an undesired end if they are found to spur a development in that specific direction. I have described this endpoint with eugenic practices that cannot be justified by clinical goals, and which – this is my principal thesis – carry the risk of harming the sense of individual autonomy as well as the moral status of persons so treated. But how should we estimate the probability that PGD and human embryonic stem cell research will set loose a dynamic that crosses the line into a positive eugenics? A desirable expansion of both our biogenetic knowledge and our genetic-technological capabilities would not be selective in the sense that they could be employed only for clinical purposes. Thus the relevant question in our context is whether the procedures of preimplantation genetic diagnosis and research on human embryonic stem cells demand the adoption of attitudes which, in their effect, tend to promote the transition from a negative to a positive eugenics.

The threshold separating negative and positive eugenics can be described in terms of a difference of *attitudes*. In the framework of clinical practice, the genetic therapist treats the living being on the basis of a justifiably assumed consensus, as if the embryo were already the second person which it will one day become. Conversely, the genetic designer assumes both an optimizing and an instrumentalizing attitude toward the embryo: the eight-cell embryo's genetic composition is to be improved according to subjective preferences. What takes the place of the performative attitude toward a future person, who in its embryonic state is already *treated as* a person who can say yes or no, is in the case of positive eugenics a hybrid combination of objectivating attitudes. I imagine a bricoleur who combines the classic goal of the breeder and aims at improving the genetic potential of a species, with the operational mode of an instrumentally acting engineer, who implements his own design and thus *works on* the embryonic cells as material. Naturally one can only speak of a 'slippery slope' insofar as there are good reasons for assuming that (a) PGD, and (b) research on human embryonic stem cells clear the path for the habituation of just these two attitudes, which are tied to the *improvement* and the *reification* of prepersonal human life.

(5a) The action context of which PGD is part makes both of these attitudes visible. Unlike cases of unwanted pregnancy, here the protection of the life of the embryo does not compete with the woman's right to self-determination. Instead it is a situation in which parents who want to have their own child start with a conditional decision. They know from the beginning that, following the diagnosis, they either have to choose among several options, or must make a binary decision between the implantation or the destruction of just one embryo. This already betrays an *intention to improvement*. The selection is based on a judgment of the quality of a human being and therefore expresses a desire for genetic optimization. An act that in the end leads to the selection of a healthier organism issues from the same attitude as a eugenic praxis.

By strictly limiting the procedure of PGD toward the goal of preventing serious genetic diseases, the parallel with negative eugenics (unobjectionable in itself, let us assume) certainly arises. Parents can claim to decide to spare an unborn child an unbearably burdened, indeed a tormented existence from a compassionate interest for the child itself. Under this description, the protection of the life of the embryo is as it were limited by the anticipated no of the unborn person himself or herself. This self-understanding seems to indicate a clinical attitude – at least not an attitude that aims at optimization. But is a clinical attitude in fact compatible with the *one-sided* and – unlike the case of negative eugenics – *irrevocable* decision between a life "worthy" or "unworthy" of living? Won't this interpretation always remain hostage to an ambiguity: the altruistic fig leaf covering the egocentricity of a wish that was conditioned from the very beginning? One shall have a child of one's own, even though there are alternatives, and this child may only come into the world if it satisfies specific criteria for quality.

This self-directed suspicion is only deepened as we think through the problematic of a *reified interaction* with the embryo in vitro. The desire for children makes the parents arrange a situation in which they have *freely to dispose*, on the basis of a scientific prognosis, over the termination or continuation of a prepersonal human life. This instrumentalization is an unavoidable part of the situation once preimplantation genetic diagnosis is permitted. If we consider the matter scrupulously, can the preference for a healthy child of one's own overrule the embryo's right to life?

(5b)   Research on human embryonic stem cells does not fit into the same perspective of breeding and self-optimization. But it does require, from the very beginning, an instrumentalizing attitude toward the "embryonic cell line." Certainly, the experimental and "applied" effort doesn't aim at a possible birth at all; thus it cannot *fail* to meet the expectation to maintain a clinical attitude toward a future person. Rather the action context is structured by the goals of the growth of knowledge and technical development. So it falls, as Ludwig Siep emphasizes, under a different description. If embryonic stem cells are manufactured, investigated, and processed in the pursuit of such ends, it is a matter of *another kind* of praxis than the reproduction (and the selection or genetic modification) of a being to be born. But this point only con-

firms the claim that tips the scales for the "slippery slope" argument: that this research praxis requires a reifying mode of operation, and therefore the same attitude toward prepersonal human life that characterizes eugenic practices.

To be sure, with the freedom of science and research a competing right comes into play and, with the collective good of health, a high-ranking value. This fact demands the usual kind of balancing, the result of which will depend on how we assess the pacemaking role of research in human embryonic stem cells for the very mode of how to use new genetic technologies. The minority in the German National Council of Ethics, which on principle rejects "the instrumentalization of the embryo for ends foreign to it," goes even a step further in the slippery-slope argument, and emphasizes the symbolic function of the protection of human embryos for all "who are not able to protect themselves and therewith not able to argue in their own defense."

In addition, we should not overestimate the weight of two further arguments, put forward by the majority who advocate permission only for the importation of excess embryonic stem cells. Morally regarded, it makes no serious difference whether one uses "excess" embryos for research purposes, or whether one manufactures them for the express purpose of this instrumentalization. From a political viewpoint, it may well be that limiting research to the importation of already available stem cells serves the purpose of keeping the scope and the duration of these researches under control. But the restrictive conditions that the National Council of Ethics recommends remain plausible only under the presupposition that we do not regard this kind of research as quite kosher. Which means compromising an issue that does not allow for any compromise. As to the other argument, I have no opinion on the controversy among experts regarding the point at which the embryo ceases to be totipotent. I only want to suggest that the distinction between pluripotent and totipotent human embryonic stem cells becomes unimportant in the present context, once we start from the premise (as do the majority of the Council who are generally in support of the controversial kind of stem cell research) that the constitution only grants a gradated protection of prepersonal human life. Pluripotent stem cells, from which human individuals can no longer develop, fall under this conception as well.

Faith and Knowledge

When restricted in one's choice of a subject by the depressing current events, one is severely tempted to compete with the John Waynes among us intellectuals to see who is the fastest shot. Only the other day, opinions differed about another issue – the question of whether, and how, we should, via genetic engineering, submit to self-instrumentalization or even pursue the goal of self-optimization. The first steps on this path led to a clash between the spokespersons of institutionalized science and those of the churches. One side feared obscurantism and the consolidation, based on skepticism toward science, of remnants of archaic emotions; the other side objected to the crude naturalism of a scientistic belief in progress supposedly undermining morality. But on September 11, 2001, the tension between secular society and religion exploded in an entirely different way.

As we now know from Atta's testament and from Bin Laden himself, the suicidal murderers who made living bombs of civil aircraft, directing them against the capitalist citadels of Western civilization, were motivated by religious beliefs. For them, the symbols of globalized modernity are an embodiment of the Great Satan. And we, too, the universal eyewitnesses of the "apocalyptic" events, were assailed by biblical images as we watched television repeat again and again, in a kind of masochistic

101

attitude, the images of the crumbling Manhattan twin towers. And the language of retaliation – which the President of the United States was not the only one to resort to in response to the unbelievable – had an Old Testament ring to it. As if the blind fundamentalist attack had struck a religious chord in the very heart of secular society, synagogues, churches, and mosques everywhere began to fill. The hidden correspondence, however, failed to induce the civil-religious mourning congregation, gathering in the New York Stadium a week later, to assume a symmetrical attitude of hatred. For all its patriotism, not a single voice was heard calling for a warlike extension of national criminal law.[1]

In spite of its religious language, fundamentalism is an exclusively modern phenomenon and, therefore, not only a problem of others. What was immediately striking about the Islamic assailants was the perceptible time-lag between their motives and their means. This mirrors the time-lag between culture and society, which in their home countries has only come to exist as the result of an accelerated and radically uprooting modernization. What in our countries, under more propitious conditions, could after all be experienced as a process of *creative* destruction was, there, not bound up with the promise of compensation for the pain suffered through the disintegration of traditional forms of life. The prospect of seeing one's material conditions of life improved is but one thing. What is crucial is the shift in mentality, perhaps blocked so far by feelings of humiliation, which in the political realm comes to be expressed in the separation of church and state. Even in Europe, where under similar circumstances history allowed for much more time to be taken in developing a sensitive attitude toward Janus-faced modernity, feelings toward "secularization" are still highly ambivalent, as shown by the dispute over genetic engineering.

Orthodoxies exist in the Western world as well as in the Middle or Far East, among Christians and Jews as well as among Muslims. If we want to avoid a clash of civilizations, we must keep in mind that the dialectic of our own occidental process of secularization has as yet not come to a close. The "war against terrorism" is no war, and what comes to be expressed in terrorism is also the fatally speechless clash of worlds, which have to work out a common language beyond the mute violence of terrorists or missiles. Faced with a globalization imposing itself via deregulated markets, many of us hoped for a return of the political in a different form – not in the original Hobbesian form of the globalized security state, that is, in its dimensions of police activity, secret service, and the military, but as a worldwide civilizing force. What we are left with, for the moment, is little more than the bleak hope for a cunning of reason – and for some self-reflection. The rift of speechlessness strikes home, too. Only if we realize what secularization means in our own postsecular societies can we be far-sighted in our response to the risks involved in a secularization miscarrying in other parts of the world. Such is the intention which guides my taking up, once more, the topic of "Faith and Knowledge." I will speak neither on bioethics nor on a new kind of terrorism but on secularization in our postsecular societies. This self-reflection is one among several steps necessary if we want to present a different image of the West to other cultures. We do not want to be perceived as crusaders of a competing religion or as salespeople of instrumental reason and destructive secularization.

Secularization in postsecular society

In Europe, the term "secularization" first had the juridical meaning of a forced conveyance of church property to the secular state. This meaning was then extended to cover the rise and development of cultural and social modernity as a whole. Ever since, "secularization" has been subject to contrasting evaluations, depending on whether its main feature is seen as the successful *taming* of clerical authority, or as the act of unlawful *appropriation*. According to the first reading – "taming" – religious ways of thinking and forms of life are *replaced* by rational, in any case superior, equivalents; whereas in the second reading – "stealing" – these modern ways of thinking and forms of life are *discredited* as illegitimately appropriated goods. The replacement model suggests a progressivist interpretation in terms of disenchanted modernity, while the expropriation model leads to an interpretation in terms of a theory of decline, that is, unsheltered modernity. Both readings make the same mistake. They construe secularization as a kind of zero-sum game between the capitalistically unbridled productivity of science and technology on the one hand, and the conservative forces of religion and the church on the other hand. Gains on one side can only be achieved at the expense of the other side, and by liberal rules which act in favor of the driving forces of modernity.

This image is inconsistent with a postsecular society which adapts to the fact that religious communities continue to exist in a context of ongoing secularization. It obscures the civilizing role of a democratically shaped and enlightened common sense that makes its way as a third party, so to speak, amid the *Kulturkampf* confusion of competing voices. To be sure, from the perspective of the liberal state, only those religious communities which abstain, by their own lights, from violence in spreading their beliefs and imposing them on their own members, let alone manipulation inducing suicide attacks, deserve the predicate of "reasonable."[2] This restraint results from a triple reflection of the believers on their position in a pluralist society. Religious consciousness must, first, come to terms with the cognitive dissonance of encountering other denominations and religions. It must, second, adapt to the authority of the sciences which hold the societal monopoly of secular knowledge. It must, last, agree to the premises of a constitutional state grounded in a profane morality. Without this thrust of reflection, monotheisms in relentlessly modernized societies unleash a destructive potential. The term "thrust of reflection" [*Reflexionsschub*] suggests, however, the misleading image of a process carried out by one side only, and of one that has already come to a close. Actually, this reflection sets in again and again, and continues with each conflict of existential weight.

As soon as an issue of existential relevance makes it to the political agenda, citizens, whether believers or unbelievers, clash over beliefs impregnated by different worldviews; grappling with the strident dissonances of public dispute, they experience the offensive fact of an antagonistic coexistence of competing worldviews. If, aware of their own fallibility, they learn to deal with this fact of pluralism in a nonviolent way, that is, without disrupting the social cohesion of a political community, they realize what the secular grounds for the separation of religion from politics in a postsecular society actually mean. The neutral state, confronted with competing claims of knowledge and faith, abstains from prejudging political decisions in favor of one side or the other. The pluralized reason of the public of citizens follows a dynamic of secularization only insofar as the latter urges equal distance to be kept, *in the outcome*, from any strong traditions and comprehensive worldviews. In its willingness to learn, however, democratic common sense remains osmotically open to *both* sides, science and religion, without relinquishing its independence.

Science as an agent of informed common sense

Of course, common sense, being full of illusions about the world, needs to be informed, without any reservation, by the sciences. The scientific theories which intrude upon the lifeworld, however, do not essentially touch on the *framework* of our everyday knowledge, which is linked to the self-understanding of speakers and actors. Learning something new about the world, and about ourselves as

105

beings in the world, changes the *content* of our self-understanding. Copernicus and Darwin revolutionized the geocentric and the anthropocentric worldview. As it is, the traces left by the destruction of the astronomical illusion about the orbits of the stars are less profound than those of the biological disillusionment about the position of man in natural history. The closer scientific findings approach our bodily existence, the more disconcerting they seem for our self-understanding. Brain research instructs us on the physiology of consciousness. But does it also change the intuitive awareness of authorship and responsibility which accompanies all our actions?

We realize what is at stake if, with Max Weber, we look at the beginnings of the "disenchantment of the world." To the extent that nature is made accessible to objectivating observation and causal explanation, it is depersonalized. Nature as an object of science is no longer part of the social frame of reference of persons who communicate and interact with one another and mutually ascribe intentions and motives. What, then, will become of these persons if they progressively subsume *themselves* under scientific descriptions? Will common sense, in the end, consent to being not only instructed, but completely absorbed by counterintuitive scientific knowledge? The philosopher Wilfrid Sellars addressed this question in 1960 (in a famous essay on "Philosophy and the Scientific Image of Man"), responding to it by the scenario of a society where the old-fashioned language games of our everyday life are invalidated in favor of the objectivating description of mental processes.

The vanishing point of this naturalization of the mind is a scientific image of man drawn up in the extensional concepts of physics, neurophysiology, or evolutionary theory, and resulting in a complete desocialization of our self-understanding as well. This naturalization of the mind can only be achieved, however, if the intentionality of human consciousness and the normativity of our actions are completely accounted for by such an objectivating self-description. The theories required would have to explain, for instance, how actors may follow, or break, rules, be they grammatical, conceptual, or moral.[3] Sellars's followers misconstrued the aporetic thought experiment of their teacher as a research program.[4] The project of a scientific "modernization" of our everyday psychology[5] led to attempts at a semantics – teleosemantics – explaining the contents of thought in terms of biology.[6] But even these most advanced efforts fail, it seems, because the concept of purposefulness with which we invest the Darwinian language game of mutation and adaptation, selection and survival is too poor to be adequate to the difference of "is" and "ought" which is implied if we violate rules – misapplying a predicate or violating a moral rule.[7]

In describing how a person did something she did not want to do, nor should have done, we *describe* her – but not in the same way as we describe a scientific object. The description of persons tacitly includes elements of the pre-scientific self-understanding of speakers and actors. If we describe an event as being a person's action, we know for instance that we describe something which can be not only *explained* like a natural process, but also, if need be, justified. In the background, there is the image of persons who may call upon one another to account for themselves, who are naturally involved in normatively regulated interactions and encounter one another in a universe of public reasons.

This perspective, going along with everyday life, explains the difference between the language games of justification and *mere* description. Even nonreductionist strategies of explanation end up against this dualism.[8] They too, after all, provide descriptions from the observer's perspective. But the participant's perspective of our everyday consciousness – in which the justificatory practices of research are grounded – can neither be easily integrated nor simply subordinated to the perspective of the observer. In our everyday dealings, we focus on others whom we address as a second person. Understanding the yes or no of the other, the contestable statements we owe and expect from one another, is bound up with this attitude toward second persons. The awareness of authorship implying accountability is the core of our self-understanding, disclosed only to the perspective of a participant, but eluding revisionary scientific description. The scientistic belief in a science which will one day not only supplement, but *replace* the self-understanding of actors as persons by an objectivating self-description is not science, but bad philosophy. No science will relieve common sense, even if scientifically informed, of the task of forming a judgment, for instance, on how we should deal with prepersonal human life under descriptions of molecular biology that make genetic interventions possible.

Democratic common sense and religion

Thus, common sense is linked to the awareness of actors who can take initiatives, and make and correct mistakes. Against the sciences, it holds its own by persisting in its perspective. The same awareness of being autonomous which eludes naturalistic reduction is also the reason for keeping a distance, on the other hand, from a religious tradition whose normative substance we nevertheless feed on. By its insistence on rational justification, science seems in the end to succeed in getting on its side an informed common sense which has found its place in the edifice of the constitutional state. Of course, the contractualist tradition, too, has religious roots – roots in the very revolution of the ways of thinking that were brought about by the ascent of the great world religions. But this legitimation of law and politics in terms of modern natural law feeds on religious sources that have long since become secularized. Against religion, the democratic common sense insists on reasons which are acceptable not just for the members of *one* religious community. Therefore, the liberal state makes believers suspect that occidental secularization might be a one-way street bypassing religion as marginal.

The other side of religious freedom is in fact a pacification of the pluralism of worldviews that distribute burdens unequally. To date, only citizens committed to religious beliefs are required to split up their identities, as it were, into their public and private elements. They are the ones who have to translate their religious beliefs into a secular language before their arguments have any chance of gaining majority support. In Germany, just to give an example, Catholics and Protestants claim the status of a subject of human rights for the gamete fertilized ex utero; this is how they engage in an attempt (an unfortunate one, I think) to translate man's likeness to God into the secular language of the constitution. But only if the secular side, too, remains sensitive to the force of articulation inherent in religious languages will the search for reasons that aim at universal acceptability not lead to an unfair exclusion of religions from the public sphere, nor sever secular society from important resources of meaning. In any event, the boundaries between secular and religious reasons are fluid. Determining these disputed boundaries should therefore be seen as a cooperative task which requires *both* sides to take on the perspective of the other one.

Liberal politics must abstain from externalizing the perpetual dispute over the secular self-awareness of society, that is, from relegating it only to the religious segment of the population. Democratic common sense is not singular; it describes the mental state of a *many-voiced* public. Secular majorities must not reach decisions in such questions before the objections of opponents who feel that these decisions violate their beliefs have been heard; they have to consider these objections as a kind of dilatory plea in order to examine what may be learned from them. Considering the religious origins of its moral foundation, the liberal state should be aware of the possibility that Hegel's "culture of common sense" ["Kultur des gemeinen Menschenverstands"] may, in view of entirely novel challenges, fail to be up to the level of articulation which characterized its own origins. Today, the all-pervasive language of the market puts all interpersonal relations under the constraint of an egocentric orientation toward one's own preferences. The social bond, however, being made up of mutual recognition, cannot be spelled out in the concepts of contract, rational choice, and maximal benefit alone.[9]

Therefore, Kant refused to let the categorical "ought" be absorbed by the whirlpool of enlightened self-interest. He enlarged subjective freedom [*Willkür*] to autonomy (or free will), thus giving the first great example – after metaphysics – of a secularizing, but at the same time salvaging, deconstruction of religious truths. With Kant, the authority of divine commands is unmistakably echoed in the unconditional validity of moral duties. With his concept of autonomy, to be sure, he destroys the traditional image of men as children of God.[10] But he preempts the trivial consequences of such a deflation by a critical *assimilation* of religious contents. His further attempt to translate the notion of "radical evil" from biblical language into the language of rational religion may seem less convincing. The unrestrained way in which this biblical heritage is once more dealt with today shows that we still lack an adequate concept for the semantic difference between what is morally wrong and what is profoundly evil. There is no devil, but the fallen archangel still wreaks havoc – in the perverted good of the monstrous deed, but also in the unrestrained urge for retaliation that promptly follows.

Secular languages which only eliminate the substance once intended leave irritations. When sin was converted to culpability, and the breaking of divine commands to an offense against human laws, something was lost. The wish for forgiveness is still bound up with the unsentimental wish to undo the harm inflicted on others. What is even more disconcerting is the irreversibility of *past* sufferings – the injustice inflicted on innocent people who were abused, debased, and murdered, reaching far beyond any extent of reparation within human power. The lost hope for resurrection is keenly felt as a void. Horkheimer's justified skepticism – "The slaughtered are really slaughtered" – with which he countered Benjamin's emphatic, or rather excessive, hope for the anamnestic power of reparation inherent in human remembrance, is far from denying the helpless impulse to change what cannot be changed any more. The exchange of letters between Benjamin and Horkheimer dates from spring 1937. Both, the true impulse and its impotence, were prolonged after the holocaust by the practice, as necessary as it was hopeless, of "coming to terms with the past" ["Aufarbeitung der Vergangenheit"] (Adorno). They are manifest as well in the rising lament over the inappropriateness of this practice. In moments like these, the unbelieving sons and daughters of modernity seem to believe that they owe more to one another, and need more for themselves, than what is accessible to them, in translation, of religious tradition – as if the semantic potential of the latter was still not exhausted.

Dispute over a heritage: philosophy versus religion

The history of German philosophy since Kant can be perceived in terms of a trial on this disputed heritage. By the end of the Middle Ages, the Hellenization of Christianity had resulted in a symbiosis of religion and metaphysics. This symbiosis was broken up again by Kant. He draws a sharp line between the moral belief of rational religion and the positive belief in revealed truths. From this perspective faith had certainly contributed to the "bettering of the soul" [Seelenbesserung], but "with its appendages of statutes and observances . . . bit by bit . . . became a fetter."[11] To Hegel, this is pure "dogmatism of enlightenment" ["Dogmatismus der Aufklärung"]. He derides the

111

Pyrrhic victory of a reason which resembles those barbarians who are victorious, but succumb to the spirit of the conquered nation, in that it holds "the upper hand outwardly" only ["der äußeren Herrschaft nach die Oberhand behält"].[12] So, with Hegel, *delimiting* reason is replaced by a reason which *embraces*. Hegel makes death by crucifixion as suffered by the Son of God the center of a way of thinking that seeks to incorporate the positive form of Christianity. God's incarnation symbolizes the life of the philosophical spirit. Even the absolute must realize itself in its other because it will experience itself as absolute power only if it passes through the agonizing negativity of self-limitation. Thus, religious contents are saved in terms of philosophical concepts. But Hegel sacrifices together with sacred history [*Heilsgeschichte*] the promise of a salvaging future in exchange for a world process revolving *in itself*. Teleology is finally bent back into a circle.

Hegel's students and followers break with the fatalism of this dreary prospect of an eternal recurrence of the same. Rather than save religion in thought, they want to realize its profanized contents in a political effort of solidary praxis. This pathos of a desublimated earthly realization of the Kingdom of God is the driving force behind the critique of religion from Feuerbach and Marx to Bloch, Benjamin, and Adorno: "Nothing of theological content will persist without being transformed; every content will have to put itself to the test of migrating into the realm of the secular, the profane" ["Nichts an theologischem Gehalt wird unverwandelt fortbestehen; ein jeglicher wird der Probe sich stellen müssen, ins Säkulare, Profane einzuwandern"].[13] Meanwhile, it is true, it had become evident from the course of history that such a project was asking too much of reason. As reason was despairing of itself under these excessive demands, Adorno secured, albeit with a purely methodological intention, the help of the Messianic perspective: "Knowledge has no light but that shed on the world by redemption" ["Erkenntnis hat kein Licht als das von der Erlösung her auf die Welt

112

scheint"].[14] What applies to Adorno here is a proposition by Horkheimer aiming at Critical Theory as a whole: "Knowing there is no God, it nevertheless believes in him" ["Sie weiß, dass es keinen Gott gibt, und doch glaubt sie an ihn"].[15] Today, Jacques Derrida, from different premises, comes to a similar position – a worthy winner of the Adorno Prize also in this respect. All he wants to retain of Messianism is "messianicity, stripped of everything."[16]

The borders of philosophy and religion, however, are mined grounds. *Reason which disclaims itself* is easily tempted to merely borrow the authority, and the air, of a sacred that has been deprived of its core and become anonymous. With Heidegger, devotion [*Andacht*] mutates to become remembrance [*Andenken*]. But there is no new insight to be gained by having the day of the Last Judgement evaporate to an undetermined event in the history of being. If posthumanism is to be fulfilled in the return to the archaic beginnings *before* Christ and *before* Socrates, the hour of religious kitsch has come. Then the department stores of art open their doors to altars from all over the world, with priests and shamans flown in from all four points of the compass for exclusive exhibitions. *Profane*, but *nondefeatist* reason, by contrast, has too much respect for the glowing embers, rekindled time and again by the issue of theodicy, to offend religion. It knows that the profanation of the sacred begins with those world religions which disenchanted magic, overcame myth, sublimated sacrifice, and disclosed the secret. Thus, it can keep its distances from religion without ignoring its perspective.

The example of genetic engineering

This ambivalence may also lead to the reasonable attitude of keeping one's distance from religion without closing one's mind to the perspective it offers. This attitude may help set the right course for the self-enlightenment of a civil society torn by *Kulturkampf*. Postsecular society continues the work, for religion itself, that religion did for myth. Not in the hybrid intention of a hostile takeover, to be sure, but out of a concern to counteract the insidious entropy of the scarce resource of meaning in its own realm. Democratic common sense must fear the media-induced indifference and the mindless conversational trivialization of all differences that make a difference. Those moral feelings which only religious language has as yet been able to give a sufficiently differentiated expression may find universal resonance once a salvaging formulation turns up for something almost forgotten, but implicitly missed. The mode for nondestructive secularization is translation. This is what the Western world, as the worldwide secularizing force, may learn from its own history. If it presents this complex image of itself to other cultures in a credible way, intercultural relations may find a language other than that of the military and the market alone.

In the controversy, for instance, about the way to deal with human embryos, many voices still evoke the first book of Moses, Genesis 1: 27: "So God created man in his own image, in the image of God created he him." In order to understand what *Gottesebenbildlichkeit* – "in the likeness of God" – means, one need not believe that the God who is love creates, with Adam and Eve, free creatures who are like him. One knows that there can be no love without recognition of the self in the other, nor freedom without mutual recognition. So, the other who has human form must himself be free in order to be able to return God's affection. In spite of his likeness to God, however, this other is also imagined as being God's creature. Regarding his origin, he cannot be of equal birth with God. This *creatural nature* of the image expresses an intuition which in the present context may even speak to those who are tone-deaf to religious connotations. Hegel had a feeling for this difference between divine "creation" and mere "coming from" God. God remains a "God of free men" only as long as we do not level out the absolute difference that exists between the creator and the creature. Only then, the fact that God gives form to human life does not imply a determination interfering with man's self-determination.

Because he is both in one, God the Creator and God the Redeemer, this creator does not need, in his actions, to abide by the laws of nature like a technician, or by the rules of a code like a biologist or computer scientist. From the very beginning, the voice of God calling into life communicates within a morally sensitive universe. Therefore God may "determine" man in the sense of enabling and, at the same time, obliging him to be free. Now, one need not believe in theological premises in order to understand what follows from this, namely, that an entirely different kind of dependence, perceived as a causal one, becomes involved if the difference assumed as inherent in the concept of creation were to disappear, and the place of God be taken by a peer – if, that is, a human being would intervene, according to his own preferences and without being justified in assuming, at least counterfactually, a consent of the concerned other, in the random combination of the parents' sets of chromosomes. This reading leads to the question I have dealt with elsewhere: Would not the first human being to determine, *at his own discretion*, the natural essence of another human being at the same time destroy the equal freedoms that exist among persons of equal birth in order to ensure their difference?

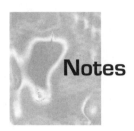

Notes

Where a German-language source is given, quotations have been translated specifically for this edition.

Are There Postmetaphysical Answers to the Question: What is the "Good Life"?

1 Theodor Adorno, *Minima Moralia: Reflections from Damaged Life*, trans. E. F. N. Jephcott (London: New Left Books, 1974), p. 15.

2 I would like to recognize the debt I owe to my friend Dick Bernstein for the extraordinary sensitivity of his many constructive critical comments over the last three decades. In the present context compare our exchange on the controversial issue of the priority of the Right over the Good, in *Habermas on Law and Democracy: Critical Exchanges*, ed. M. Rosenfield and A. Arato (Berkeley: University of California Press, 1998), pp. 287–305 and 384–9.

3 A. Mitscherlich, *Freiheit und Unfreiheit in der Krankheit, Studien zur psychosomatischen Medizin* 3 (Frankfurt am Main: Suhrkamp, 1977), p. 128.

4 S. Kierkegaard, *Either/Or*, part 2, ed. and trans. H. V. Hong and E. H. Hong, in *Kierkegaard's Writings*, vol. 4 (Princeton: Princeton University Press, 1987), p. 260.

5 S. Kierkegaard, *The Sickness unto Death*, ed. and trans. H. V. Hong and E. H. Hong, in *Kierkegaard's Writings*, vol. 19 (Princeton: Princeton University Press, 1980), p. 90.

6 S. Kierkegaard, *Philosophical Fragments*, ed. and trans. H. V. Hong and E. H. Hong, in *Kierkegaard's Writings*, vol. 7 (Princeton: Princeton University Press, 1985), p. 111.
7 Kierkegaard, *Sickness unto Death*, pp. 52–3.
8 Ibid., p. 14.
9 M. Theunissen, *Das Selbst auf dem Grund der Verzweiflung* (Frankfurt am Main: Athenäum, 1991), in English as *Kierkegaard's Concept of Despair* (Princeton: Princeton University Press, Forthcoming).
10 Kierkegaard, *Philosophical Fragments*, p. 45.
11 H. Plessner, *Laughing and Crying: A Study of the Limits of Human Behavior*, trans. J. S. Churchill and M. Greene (Evanston: Northwestern University Press, 1970), pp. 27–32.
12 Treaty of Nice, *Official Journal of the European Communities* (2000), C80/1.

The Debate on the Ethical Self-Understanding of the Species

Epigraph from Andreas Kuhlmann, *Politik des Lebens, Politik des Sterbens* (Berlin: Alexander Fest Verlag, 2001).

1 R. Kollek, I. Schneider, "Verschwiegene Interessen," *Süddeutsche Zeitung*, July 5, 2001. For background information on how political acceptance of embryonic research was solicited, see C. Schwägerl, "Die Geister, die sie riefen," *FAZ*, June 16, 2001.
2 I will not go into the more specific questions of the moral responsibility we would have to take, with respect to a possible modification of the germ line, for the far-reaching intergenerational effects of germ line therapy (banned, as yet), or even for the secondary effects of body cell therapy; cf. M. Lappé, "Ethical Issues in Manipulating the Human Germ Line," in H. Kuhse and P. Singer (eds), *Bioethics* (Oxford: Blackwell, 1999), pp. 155–64. In the following, I will refer, without further specification, to "genetic interventions" which are carried out before birth.
3 N. Agar, "Liberal Eugenics," in Kuhse and Singer, *Bioethics*, p. 173: "Liberals doubt that the notion of disease is up for

the moral theoretic task the therapeutic/eugenic distinction requires of it."

4   Johannes Rau, "Der Mensch ist jetzt Mitspieler der Evolution geworden," *FAZ*, May 19, 2001.

5   I agree with colleagues who think the biosciences capable of rapid achievements also usable for biotechnology: "Science so often confounds the best predictions, and we should not risk finding ourselves unprepared for the genetic engineer's equivalent of Hiroshima. Better to have principles covering impossible situations than no principles for situations that are suddenly upon us" (Agar, "Liberal Eugenics," p. 172).

6   R. Kollek, *Präimplantationsdiagnostik* (Tübingen: A.Francke, 2000), p. 214.

7   Andreas Kuhlmann, *Politik des Lebens, Politik des Sterbens* (Berlin: Alexander Fest Verlag, 2001), pp. 104ff.

8   James D. Watson, "Die Ethik des Genoms. Warum wir Gott nicht mehr die Zukunft des Menschen überlassen dürfen," *FAZ*, Sept. 26, 2000.

9   See the illuminating commentary by Thomas Assheuer, "Der Künstliche Mensch," *Die Zeit*, Mar. 15, 2001.

10 See *Zeit-Dokument* 2 (1999), pp. 4–15.

11 J. Habermas, *Between Facts and Norms: Contributions to a Discourse Theory of Law and Democracy*, trans. W. Rehg (Cambridge: Polity; Cambridge, Mass.: MIT Press, 1996). J. Habermas, *The Inclusion of the Other: Studies in Political Theory*, ed. C. Cronin and P. De Greiff (Cambridge: Polity; Cambridge, Mass.: MIT Press, 1999).

12 As an example, cf. the contributions to the debate among philosophers in *Die Zeit*, nos 4–10 (2001).

13 The intense exchange of ideas with Lutz Wingert and Rainer Forst was very helpful. My thanks also go to Tilman Habermas for his detailed comments. Of course, each of these advisers has specific reservations. My own concern the fact that I address this issue without originally being familiar with the field of bioethics. I therefore regret that I came upon the study by Allen Buchanan, Daniel W. Brock, Norman Daniels and Daniel Wikler, *From Chance to Choice: Genetics and Justice* (Cambridge: Cambridge University Press, 2000), only after having concluded my manuscript. I share their deontological perspective of judgment. As for

the dissensus that nevertheless remains, I can only outline it by resorting to a few additional notes.

14 W. van den Daele, "Die Natürlichkeit des Menschen als Kriterium und Schranke technischer Eingriffe," *Wechsel-Wirkung*, June–Aug. (2000), pp. 24–31.

15 Ibid., p. 25.

16 W. van den Daele, "Die Moralisierung der menschlichen Natur und die Naturbezüge in gesellschaftlichen Institutionen," *Kritische Vierteljahrbuch für Gesetzgebung und Rechtswissenschaft* 2 (1978), pp. 351–66.

17 Ulrich Beck, *Risk Society*, trans. M. Ritter (London: Sage, 1992); J. Habermas, "Conceptions of Modernity: A Look Back at Two Traditions," in Habermas, *The Postnational Constellation: Political Essays*, ed. and trans. Max Pensky (Cambridge: Polity; Cambridge, Mass.: MIT Press, 2001).

18 L. Honnefelder, "Die Herausforderung des Menschen durch die Genomforschung Gentechnik," *Forum (Info der Bundeszentrale für gesundheitliche Aufklärung)* 1 (2000), p. 49.

19 For the reasons indicated above, I will focus on the fundamental question of whether we may want to take any steps at all toward liberal eugenics. I will not go into questions of the just way of implementing such procedures. The normative problems arising as a consequence of eugenics being principally welcomed are addressed, in the perspective of Rawls's theory of justice, by Buchanan et al., *From Chance to Choice*, p. 4: "The primary objective of this book is . . . to answer a single question: What are the most basic moral principles that would guide public policy and individual choice concerning the use of genetic interventions in a just and humane society in which the powers of genetic intervention are much more developed than they are today."

20 R. Dworkin, "Die falsche Angst, Gott zu spielen," *Zeit-Dokument* (1999), p. 39; cf. also "Playing God: Genes, Clones, and Luck," in R. Dworkin, *Sovereign Virtue: The Theory and Practice of Equality* (Cambridge: Harvard University Press, 2000), pp. 427–52.

21 I will refrain, in the present context, from going into the juridical dispute over the implications of the present jurisdiction in Germany concerning Article 218 StGB (abortion). There is a decision of the Federal Constitutional Court with regard to the legal protection of prenatal life

from the moment of nidation. Whether this decision can be applied without further qualification, as Herta Däubler-Gmelin and Ernst Benda assume, to human life as being entitled to absolute protection from the moment of fertilization is controversial among legal experts, and seems questionable to me, as well; cf. M. Pawlik, "Der Staat hat dem Embryo alle Trümpfe genommen," *FAZ*, June 27, 2001. As to a comparison of various juridical decisions, see the informative essay by R. Erlinger, "Von welchem Zeitpunkt an ist der Embryo juristisch geschützt?" *Süddeutsche Zeitung*, July 4, 2001. Incidentally, interpretation of the constitution is a long-term learning process which, time and again, has induced the supreme courts to correct their own previous decisions. If existing legal positions are confronted, in the light of other historical circumstances, with new moral reasons, the constitutional principles – being themselves morally grounded – require that the law follows moral arguments.

22 Cf. R. Merkel, "Rechte für Embryonen?" *Die Zeit*, Jan. 25, 2001; U. Mueller, "Gebt uns die Lizenz zum Klonen!" *FAZ*, Mar. 9, 2001.

23 R. Dworkin, *Life's Dominion: An Argument about Abortion and Euthanasia* (London: HarperCollins, 1993).

24 This is taken into account by the Aristotelian-scholastic doctrine of soul being only successively bestowed, cf. the survey by H. Schmoll, "Wann wird der Mensch ein Mensch?" *FAZ*, May 31, 2001.

25 M. Nussbaum criticizes Kant's distinction between the intelligible and the physical existence of the acting person: "What's wrong with Kant's distinction? . . . It ignores the fact that our dignity is that of a certain sort of animal; it is a dignity that could not be possessed by a being who was not mortal and vulnerable, just as the beauty of a cherry tree in bloom could not be possessed by a diamond." "Disabled Lives: Who Cares?" *New York Review of Books*, Jan. 11, 2001.

26 George Herbert Mead's fundamental insight is shared by Helmuth Plessner and Arnold Gehlen.

27 Hannah Arendt has pointed to "plurality" as a fundamental characteristic of human existence. The life of a human being proceeds only on condition that there is interaction

with other human beings: "For human beings, to live means – according to the expression in Latin, the language of the people who are perhaps the most profoundly political we know – 'to be among men' (inter homines esse), and to die, 'to cease to be among men' (desinere inter homines esse)" (H. Arendt, *Vita Activa* (Munich, 1959), p. 15; see Arendt, *The Human Condition* (Chicago: Chicago University Press, 1958).

28 Being *endowed* with reason means that birth, the moment of our entry into the social world, at the same time marks the moment from which the *capacity* of being a person can be realized, no matter in which form. Even a comatose patient participates in this form of life. Cf. M. Seel, *Ethisch-Ästhetische Studien* (Frankfurt am Main, 1996), pp. 215ff.: "Therefore morality treats all members of the human species as beings wanting life as a person, irrespective of the degree to which they are actually capable of leading such a life . . . The respect of the integrity of the other, established in the mutual recognition of persons, must apply to all human beings without exception; they all have the same fundamental right to participation in life as a person, irrespective of the degree to which they have (at all or temporarily) the capacity of self-determined participation. The core of morality can only be the most simple one, that is, to treat all human beings as human beings."

29 L. Wingert, *Gemeinsinn und Moral* (Frankfurt am Main: Suhrkamp, 1993).

30 S. Rixen, "Totenwürde," *FAZ*, Mar. 13, 2001.

31 W. Kersting, "Menschenrechtsverletzung ist nicht Wertverletzung," *FAZ*, Mar. 17, 2001.

32 R. Dworkin, *Taking Rights Seriously* (London: Duckworth, 1977); K. Günther, *Der Sinn für Angemessenheit* (Frankfurt am Main: Suhrkamp, 1988), pp. 335ff.

33 O. Höffe, "Wessen Menschenwürde?" *Die Zeit*, Feb. 1, 2001.

34 For example, Buchanan et al. speak of the uncanny scenario of a "genetic communitarianism" according to which various subcultures will pursue the eugenic self-optimizing of the human species in different directions, thus jeopardizing the unity of human nature as the basis, up to now, for all human beings to understand and to mutually recognize one another: "We can no longer assume that there will be

a single successor to what has been regarded as human nature. We must consider the possibility that at some point in the future, different groups of human beings may follow divergent paths of development through the use of genetic technology. If this occurs, there will be different groups of beings, each with its own 'nature', related to one another only through a common ancestor (the human race), just as there are now different species of animals who evolved through random mutations and natural selection" (*From Chance to Choice*, pp. 177ff.).

35 I owe this decisive idea to a discussion with Lutz Wingert. He is also the author of an instructive proposal for a project to be conducted at the Kulturwissenschaftliches Institut Essen: "What makes a form of life humane? Our culture between biology and humanism."

36 It does make a difference, however, whether we apply the interpretive model of "tinkering around" to *our own* biotechnological interventions into nature, carried out under laboratory conditions, or, as for instance in F. Jakob (*Das Spiel des Möglichen*, Munich, 1983), to the evolution of nature *itself*. This distinction becomes relevant in a normative sense as soon as both are associated, by way of legitimation, in order to suggest the naturalistic fallacy of seeing biotechnology as natural evolution being continued by its own means. This reflection is based on a manuscript by P. Janich and M. Weingarten, *Verantwortung ohne Verständnis. Wie die Ethikdebatte zur Gentechnik von deren Wissenschaftstheorie abhängt* (Marburg, 2001).

37 H. Jonas, "Lasst uns einen Menschen klonieren," in Jonas, *Technik, Medizin und Eugenik. Zur Praxis des Prinzips Verantwortung* (Frankfurt am Main: Suhrkamp, 1985), p. 165.

38 Ibid., p. 168; this uncontrollability increases with interventions into the germ line, see note 2 above.

39 M. Horkheimer and T. W. Adorno, *Dialektik der Aufklärung* (Amsterdam, 1947), p. 54; in English as *Dialectic of Enlightenment*, trans. J. Cumming (London and New York: Verso, 1997).

40 Agar, "Liberal Eugenics," p. 171.

41 John Robertson, cited in ibid., pp. 172ff.

42 Ibid., p. 173. The same parallel in Buchanan et al., *From Chance to Choice*, pp. 156ff.

43   H. Plessner, *Die Stufen des Organischen* (1927), in *Gesammelte Schriften*, vol. 4 (Frankfurt am Main: Suhrkamp, 1981).

44   Tilmann Habermas, "Die Entwicklung sozialen Urteilens bei jugendlichen Magersüchtigen," *Acta Paedo-psychiatrica*, 51 (1988), pp. 147–55.

45   Buchanan et al., *From Chance to Choice*, p. 121: "Disease and impairment, both physical and mental, are construed as adverse departure from or impairments of species-typical normal functional organization . . . The line between disease and impairment and normal functioning is thus drawn in the relatively objective and non-speculative context provided by the biomedical sciences, broadly construed." The authors refer, from a normative point of view, to "normal functioning" as a "natural primary good", in an analogy to the social primary goods introduced by Rawls.

46   J. Harris, "Is Gene Therapy a Form of Eugenics," in Kuhse and Singer, *Bioethics*, p. 167: "This is important because we need an account of disability we can use for the potentially self-conscious gametes, embryos, fetuses and neonates, and for the temporarily unconscious, which does not wait on subsequent ratification by the person concerned."

47   Kuhlmann, *Politik des Lebens*, p. 17.

48   Buchanan et al., *From Chance to Choice*, pp. 90ff.

49   E. Tugendhat, *Selbstbewusstsein und Selbstbestimmung* (Frankfurt am Main, 1979), pp. 68ff., in English as *Self-Consciousness and Self-Determination*, trans. P. Stern (Cambridge, Mass.: MIT Press, 1986); B. Mauersberg, *Der lange Abschied von der Bewusstseinsphilosophie* (Frankfurt am Main: Peter Lang, 2000).

50   Arendt, *Vita Activa*, pp. 15ff.; see also Arendt, *The Human Condition*, pp. 8ff.

51   Arendt, *Vita Activa*, p. 243, and see also pp. 164f.

52   Buchanan et al., *From Chance to Choice*, pp. 177ff.: "Even if an individual is no more locked in by the effects of a parental choice than he or she would have been by unmodified nature, most of us might feel differently about accepting the results of a natural lottery versus the imposed values of our parents. The force of feeling locked in may well be different." Curiously enough, the authors bring this argu-

ment to bear only against what they term "communitarian eugenics", not against the practice of liberal eugenics in general, of which they approve.

53 Cf. above the references to Kierkegaard as the first modern ethicist.

54 See the argument of Hans Jonas in *Technik, Medizin und Eugenik*, pp. 190–3; and K. Braun, *Menschenwürde und Biomedizin* (Frankfurt am Main: Campus, 2000), pp. 162–79. Buchanan et al., *From Chance to Choice*, do take this into account, when referring to the child's "right to an open future" (postulated by Joel Feinberg in a different context: "The Child's Right to an Open Future," in W. Aiken and H. LaFollette (eds), *Whose Child? Children's Rights, Parental Authority, and State Power* (Totowa, N.J.: Littlefield, Adams, 1980)). But they believe that restriction of this right by the precursor model of a twin chronologically out of phase can only be assumed from the – erroneous – premises of genetic determinism. They fail to see that here, as in the case of enhancing eugenics, it is primarily the intention governing the eugenic intervention that counts. The person concerned knows that the manipulation has been carried out with the sole intention of acting on the phenotypic molding of a specific genetic program, and this of course on condition that the technologies required for this goal have proved to be successful.

55 Cf. my three replies in Habermas, *The Postnational Constellation*, pp. 163–72.

56 As long as the advocates of PID model their thought on the current legal conditions of medical indications for abortion, they refuse any change of perspective from what is bad for the mother's health to what is bad for the health of the future child.

57 Disregarding the aspect of deliberately induced selection, this procedure, too, may well involve another relevant aspect which in abortion, being a situation of a different nature, is covered by the woman's right to self-determination: whether or not parents can be reasonably supposed to cope with the situation they have to expect. The parents must believe themselves capable of coping, even under aggravated conditions, with the demanding responsibility for a child who will share their life.

58 Rainer Forst has tried to convince me, with ingenious arguments, that with this step I unnecessarily leave the path of deontological virtue.

59 J. Habermas, "Richtigkeit versus Wahrheit," in Habermas, *Wahrheit und Rechtfertigung* (Frankfurt am Main, 1999), pp. 271–318, here at pp. 313ff.; forthcoming as *Truth and Justification* (Cambridge: Polity; Cambridge, Mass.: MIT Press, 2003).

Postscript

60 The Program in Law, Philosophy, and Social Theory, New York University, Law School, Fall 2001.

61 See the contributions by Dieter Birnbacher, Ludwig Siep and Robert Spaemann in *Deutsche Zeitschrift für Philosophie*, 50, no. 1 (2002).

62 See Nationaler Ethikrat, Stellungnahme zum Import menschlicher embryonaler Stammzellen, Dezember 2001, 5.1.1: "Rechtsethische Überlegungen zum Status früher embryonaler Lebensphasen" (National Council of Ethics, position paper on the importation of human embryonic stem cells, Dec. 2001, 5.1.1: Legal-ethical reflections on the status of early stages of embryonic life).

63 J. Habermas, *Kommunikatives Handeln und detranscendentalisierte Vernunft* (Stuttgart, 2001); forthcoming in Habermas, *Truth and Justification*.

64 Seen from a religious perspective as well, the necessary beginning presupposition for a life history of one's own is that it is removed from the arbitrary will of a peer.

65 D. Birnbacher, "Habermas' ehrgeiziges Beweisziel – erreicht oder verfehlt?" (Habermas's ambitious evidentiary goal – success or failure?), *Deutsche Zeitschrift für Philosophie*, 50, no. 1 (2002).

66 I am not considering the particular problem of selection; my interest here is only the prenatal determination of gender.

67 The objection treated in section 2 above is explicable as the result of neglecting just this difference.

68 See Habermas, *Wahrheit und Rechtfertigung*, Introduction, and the contributions on the topic of "naturalism and

natural history" in *Deutsche Zeitschrift für Philosophie*, 50 (2002), pp. 857–927.

69 Georg Lohmann ("Die Herausforderung der Ethik durch Lebenswissenschaften und Medizin," MS, 2002, p. 19) characterizes this point in my argument in the following way: "The indirect *moral* connection to his *ethical* argument is able to claim a greater weight than an argument based directly on a worldview."

70 L. Siep, "Moral und Gattungsethik," *Deutsche Zeitschrift für Philosophie*, 50, no. 1 (2002).

71 R. Spaemann, "Habermas über Bioethik," *Deutsche Zeitschrift für Philosophie*, 50, no. 1 (2002).

Faith and Knowledge

1 H. Prantl, "Das Weltgericht," *Süddeutsche Zeitung*, Sept. 18, 2001.

2 J. Rawls, *Politischer Liberalismus* (Frankfurt am Main, 1998), pp. 132–41, English edition *Political Liberalism* (New York: Columbia University Press, 1993); R. Forst, "Toleranz, Gerechtigkeit, Vernunft," in Forst (ed.), *Toleranz* (Frankfurt am Main: Campus, 2000), pp. 144–61.

3 W. Sellars, *Science, Perception and Reality* (1963; Altascadero, Calif.: Ridgeview, 1991), p. 38.

4 P. M. Churchland, *Scientific Realism and the Plasticity of Mind* (Cambridge: Cambridge University Press, 1979).

5 J. D. Greenwood (ed.), *The Future of Folk Psychology: Intentionality and Cognitive Science* (Cambridge: Cambridge University Press, 1991), Introduction, pp. 1–21.

6 W. Detel, "Teleosemantik. Ein neuer Blick auf den Geist?" *Deutsche Zeitschrift für Philosophie*, 49, no. 3 (2001), pp. 465–91. Teleosemantics, based on neo-Darwinian assumptions and conceptual analyses, aims to show how the normative consciousness of living beings who use symbols and represent facts might have developed. According to this approach, the intentional frame of the human mind originates from the selective advantage of certain behaviors (e.g. the bees' dance) which are interpreted as representations by those belonging to the same species. Against the background of normalized copies of this kind, divergent behaviors are, then, supposed to be interpretable as

misrepresentations – which provides a natural explanation for the origins of normativity.

7 W. Detel, "Haben Frösche und Sumpfmenschen Gedanken? Einige Probleme der Teleosemantik," *Deutsche Zeitschrift für Philosophie*, 49, no. 4 (2001), pp. 601–26.

8 These research strategies account for the complexity of new properties (of organic life or of man) emerging on higher evolutionary stages by abstaining from describing processes of the higher evolutionary stage in concepts which apply to processes of a lower evolutionary stage.

9 A. Honneth, *The Struggle for Recognition*, trans. J. Anderson (Cambridge: Polity, 1995).

10 The Preface to the first edition of *Religion within the Limits of Reason Alone* (1793) begins with the sentence: "So far as morality is based upon the conception of man as a free agent who, just because he is free, binds himself through his reason to unconditioned laws, it stands in need neither of the idea of another Being over him, for him to apprehend his duty, nor an incentive other than the law itself, for him to do his duty" (I. Kant, *Religion within the Limits of Reason Alone*, trans. and introd. T. M. Greene and H. H. Hudson (La Salle, Ill.: Open Court, 1934), p. 3).

11 Kant, *Religion within the Limits of Reason Alone*.

12 G. W. F. Hegel, *Faith and Knowledge*, trans. W. Cerf and H. S. Harris (Albany: State University of New York Press, 1977).

13 T. W. Adorno, *Critical Models: Interventions and Catchwords*, trans. H. W. Pickford (New York: Columbia University Press, 1998), p. 136.

14 T. W. Adorno, *Minima Moralia: Reflections from Damaged Life*, trans. E. F. N. Jephcott (London: New Left Books, 1974), p. 247.

15 M. Horkheimer, "Kritische Theorie und Theologie" (Dec. 1968), pp. 507–9 of *Gesammelte Schriften*, vol. 14, at p. 508.

16 J. Derrida, "Faith and Knowledge: The Two Sources of 'Religion' at the Limits of Reason Alone," in J. Derrida and G. Vattimo (eds), *Religion* (Cambridge: Polity; Stanford: Stanford University Press, 1998), p. 18; cf. also J. Derrida, "Den Tod geben," in A. Haverkamp (ed.), *Gewalt und Gerechtigkeit* (Frankfurt am Main: Suhrkamp, 1994), pp. 331–445.